ALSO BY LAWRENCE W. TULLER

Exporting, Importing, and Beyond

Mastering Markets in South America

Strategic Marketing in the Caribbean

Strategic Marketing in Central America

Strategic Marketing in South America

Doing Business in Latin America and the Caribbean

The World Markets Desk Book

*The McGraw-Hill Handbook of Global Trade
and Investment Financing*

*Going Global: New Opportunities for Global Companies
to Compete in World Markets*

- **Negotiating contracts and agreements**

- **Understanding culture and customs**

- **Marketing products and services**

An American's Guide to Doing Business in
Latin America

Lawrence W. Tuller

A
BUSINESS
Avon, Massachusetts

Published by
Adams Business, an F+W Publications Company
57 Littlefield Street, Avon, MA 02322. U.S.A.
www.adamsmedia.com

ISBN 10: 1-59869-212-7
ISBN 13: 978-1-59869-212-9

Printed in Canada.
J I H G F E D C B A

Library of Congress Cataloging-in-Publication Data
is available from the publisher.

This publication is designed to provide accurate and authoritative information
with regard to the subject matter covered. It is sold with the understanding
that the publisher is not engaged in rendering legal, accounting, or other
professional advice. If legal advice or other expert assistance is required, the
services of a competent professional person should be sought.
　—From a *Declaration of Principles* jointly adopted by a Committee of the
American Bar Association and a Committee of Publishers and Associations

Many of the designations used by manufacturers and sellers to distinguish
their product are claimed as trademarks. Where those designations appear
in this book and Adams Media was aware of a trademark claim, the designations have been printed with initial capital letters.

Map on page 261 by Map Resources.

This book is available at quantity discounts for bulk purchases.
For information, please call 1-800-289-0963.

CONTENTS

Chapter 1

The New Latin America

Get out of the way, India. Move over, China. Stand back, Southeast Asia. Here comes the new kid on the block, a reborn Latin America. Bursting with enthusiasm. Ready to erupt with a dynamism unseen in the Western Hemisphere since the Industrial Revolution. Latin America, exuding an economic exuberance that is sure to be the envy of the developing world. And U.S. exporters have seen this coming. Last year alone they shipped four-and-a-half times as much product to this region as they did to China, twenty-four times the amount they shipped to India, and twice as much as they shipped to the United Kingdom, Germany, and France combined.

But doing business in Latin America is not easy. A constantly changing landscape makes long-term strategies especially difficult. If there is one truism about this region, it is that if you don't like the way the politics, economics, and social conditions are going now, wait 'til tomorrow and they will change.

Latin America's never-stopping politico-economic pendulum swings wildly to and fro. From dictators to freely elected presidents to elected autocrats. From liberal socialist governments to reactionary right-wing rule to populism. From hyperinflation to modest economic growth to rapidly rising prices. From shattered banking systems to stable financial markets to bank failures. From protectionist trade to free trade to the nationalization of entire industries. From isolation to open borders hungry for foreign investment to forced joint ownership of projects with government. Such a wildly swinging pendulum muddies the waters for trade and investment. Misunderstanding the North and misunderstood by the North, Latin governments and their citizens continue to ride the fringes of economic progress, unable to penetrate the psyche of either Republican or Democratic administrations in Washington.

Part of the problem is the enormous mixture of cultures that comprises Latin America and confuses Americans.

Mexico, the Caribbean nations, Central America, and South America—in fact, everything south of the U.S. border—comprise what we commonly call Latin America. Imposed by the Spanish conquerors of the sixteenth and seventeenth centuries, the Spanish language dominates the region, but other languages are also spoken. Portuguese is the official language in Brazil; it's English in Guyana, Dutch in Suriname, and French in French Guiana. In the Caribbean, English, Dutch, French, and Creole are spoken along with Spanish. In Central America, English is the language of Belize. Spanish is official in all other countries. One-third of Guatemala's population is indigenous and speaks a mixture of Mayan dialects.

Culturally, the region is equally mixed. In countries where Spanish or Portuguese is the official language, the Hispanic culture and Catholic religion inherited from Spain and Portugal are predominant. In Guyana, however, more than 50 percent of the population is descended from East Indians and practices the Indian culture and Hindu religion. In Haiti, a combination of French and African cultures has nurtured the Voodoo religion. The English-speaking Caribbean mostly consists of African descendants influenced by a European heritage, creating a unique West Indian culture that has welcomed Pentecostal preaching. Fidel Castro's atheism and its penetration of the Cuban culture is unique in the region.

In Central America, Peru, Bolivia, and Ecuador, as well as in certain parts of Brazil, mestizo is the predominant race. A mestizo is a person of mixed ancestry, especially of mixed Spanish or Portuguese and indigenous Amerindian.

Argentina is strongly influenced by descendants of settlers from Northern and Southern Europe, especially Italy and Spain. In the Caribbean, the United States owns a territory (the English-speaking Virgin Islands) and a commonwealth (Spanish-speaking Puerto Rico).

Size also matters, especially in the business world. Brazil dominates the region, with 186 million people and a geographic size equivalent to the continental United States. Its industrial base is very similar to that of the United States. Manufacturing, retail, and service industries are all healthy and growing. At the other end of the spectrum, Haiti and Nicaragua are the two poorest countries in the region with gross domestic product (GDP) per head of $1,600 and $2,400, respectively. These two countries, along with Bolivia and Suriname, stand in stark contrast to the sophisticated urban centers of São Paulo, Rio de Janeiro, Buenos Aires, Santiago, Bogotá, and Mexico City.

Political upheaval and violence have characterized Latin America for centuries. Prior to 1989, when a democratic wave washed over virtually all Latin American countries, Peru had experienced only four years of elected governments, Ecuador eight years, Brazil one year, and Uruguay barely four months. Bolivia had gone through 180 presidents in 160 years. Peronist Argentina had been little more than a police state for seventy years. Paraguay's iron-fisted president, Alfredo Stroessner, played host to thousands of Nazi war criminals. For two decades prior to 1960, Venezuela was governed by autocratic dictators. Between 1946 and 1966, more than 300,000 Colombians were killed by their own government. Even after 1989, under democratically elected governments, Brazilian police with automatic weapons wiped out scores of homeless children; Venezuelans twice rioted against their president and eventually elected a notorious autocrat; Peru's Shining Path terrorists massacred Peruvians and foreigners at will; Colombian drug gangs, protected by the army branch of the Communist party (called

Fuegas Armadas Revolucionarias de Colombia, or FARC), assassinated presidential candidates and judges, while bandits ruled mountain villages. Guatemala, El Salvador, and Nicaragua suffered years of right-wing and left-wing bloodshed, with death squads massacring indigenous tribes and squashing any and all resistance.

In such a setting, it's easy to understand why managing exports to the region, sourcing materials or parts from Latin American suppliers, or opening and operating Latin American facilities are at best difficult tasks and at worst, nightmares. But cultural mores, political upheaval, and chaotic violence are only some of the reasons that doing business there is difficult. An array of other external market forces—that is, market forces beyond the jurisdiction of corporate boardrooms and the control of company management—determines to a very large extent the types of pricing, distribution, packaging, production scheduling, employee incentives, and financing policies that will work. These external forces create market environments that are as different from those in the United States, Canada, or Europe as night is from day.

What external market forces make Latin America such a challenge? Although the magnitude of each varies from country to country, the following seem to bear most heavily on business decisions:

- Government interference
- Foreign-exchange controls
- Trade pacts
- Barely functional court systems
- Closed business cartels
- Thriving underground economies
- Antiquated banking systems
- Open corruption in both public and private sectors

These conditions create rapidly changing, confusing, and often hostile market environments that, more often than not, demand decisions at variance with your organization's domestic objectives. They cause business climates to be turbulent, unpredictable, and very unforgiving. Managerial errors are not tolerated. Latin American markets are anything but user friendly, as American markets tend to be.

Because these external forces are so powerful, marketing strategies that actually bring expected results must be broad, long term, and very flexible. You must be ready, willing, and able to make changes in pricing, distribution, packaging, promotions, and even product design as market forces dictate.

You must court government officials at various levels, sharply differentiate between social classes and gender, and adapt to cultural dissimilarities. You must take care of recalcitrant customs officials, union bosses, and influential intermediaries. And to accomplish these feats, you must work through local partners.

With such a staggering number of external forces, plus the wide range of cultures, languages, and religions, it's very difficult to look at Latin America as a single market. Instead, it must be viewed as a conglomeration of markets, peoples, and cultures, each unique, yet all similar. Each is worthy of individual assessment, yet all suffer from lack of attention from the U.S. government. Fortunately, U.S. businesses large and small look to Latin markets with increasing optimism.

To understand Latin America, one must first recognize the radical changes that have occurred since 1989. By so doing, and accepting the fact that no one in Latin America wants to turn the clock back to pre-1989 times, you will understand how economically powerful Latin America could be in the future. The Lost Decade of the 1980s was the turning point.

The Lost Decade

The turbulent, bloodletting decade of the 1970s and the so-called Lost Decade of the 1980s are in the past. The experiment in democracy of the 1990s proved at best confusing and at worst disruptive. During the early 1990s, conditions in most Latin American countries resembled the Wild West of the United States in the late nineteenth century. Political, social, economic, and financial institutions were being reinvented, while social disorder, chaotic political maneuvering, and decrepit infrastructures tore at the very fabric of the region. But the nations of Latin America survived their essay with autocratic governments, military holocausts, and protectionist economic policies. They passed through the idealistic phase of democratic ideology and began to taste the benefits and dangers of freely elected governments.

All Latin American nations are now moving toward their rightful place in the global economy. This region is no longer a backwater. Its citizens are no longer wrestling with military rule, state-controlled economies, and unworkable democratic administrations. Latin America has, indeed, evolved beyond inexperienced exuberance. In virtually all countries, political institutions, financial systems, and environmental and social awareness have matured. In fact, it's safe to say that some Latin American countries have evolved well beyond what many have called developing economies and are now approaching developed country status.

Every country except Cuba now has a working democratic government. Maybe they aren't all working as well as we would like—Venezuela, Bolivia, and Ecuador come to mind—but all heads of state and legislative bodies have been duly elected in multi-party political campaigns.

Financial institutions in most countries are relatively stable. Yes, some of the smaller Caribbean states, as well as Bolivia and Ecuador, have a way to go before their banking systems are able to handle much in the way of trade or project financing. But all nations have weathered the storm of currency devaluations. In Mexico, Argentina, Brazil, Colombia, and Chile, the capital markets and banking systems are on more solid footing today than in recent memory.

At the macroeconomic level, hyperinflation has disappeared, although in two-thirds of the region inflation is still much too high. In Argentina, Venezuela, Costa Rica, and Jamaica, high interest rates continue to delay much-needed investment in infrastructure projects and manufacturing plants. However, with stability in capital markets and the absence of new shockwaves from foreign currency devaluations, interest rates should eventually come down throughout the region. **Table 1-1** shows GDP per capita in purchasing power parities and other key statistics for each country.

According to the Organization for Economic Cooperation and Development (OECD) purchasing power parities (PPP) are "currency conversion rates that both convert to a common currency and equalize the purchasing power of different currencies. In other words, they eliminate the differences in price levels between countries in the process of conversion." Economists believe this presents a truer picture of economies than traditional GDP per-capita calculations. Perhaps PPP is a little easier to understand when one thinks of it as a mechanism to state that exchange rates between two countries are in equilibrium when the purchasing power for a given basket of goods is the same in the two countries. *The Economist* magazine issues its McDonald's Big Mac Index once a year. This hamburger index, otherwise known as the Big Mac PPP, is the exchange rate that would leave a hamburger in any country costing the same as in the United States. You can find a thorough description of the Big Mac PPP in the March 27, 2004, issue of *The Economist*.

Table 1-1 | Key Statistics

	Per Capita GDP (PPP $)	Annual Growth Rate (%)
North America		
Mexico	10,100	3.0
South America		
Argentina	13,700	8.7
Bolivia	2,700	3.4
Brazil	8,400	2.4
Chile	11,300	6.0
Colombia	7,100	4.3
Ecuador	3,900	3.0
Guyana	3,800	(2.5)
Peru	6,100	5.8
Paraguay	4,900	3.4
Uruguay	16,000	6.1
Venezuela	6,500	9.1
Central America		
Costa Rica	10,100	3.3
El Salvador	5,100	2.9
Guatemala	5,200	3.1
Honduras	2,800	4.0
Nicaragua	2,400	4.0
Panama	7,100	4.9
Caribbean (major economies only)		
Dominican Republic	6,600	6.5
Jamaica	4,200	1.5
Trinidad/Tobago	12,900	7.0

Source: Bureau of Public Affairs, U.S. Department of State, 2004 and 2005; CIA World Factbook

Literacy (%)	Population (Millions)	Inflation Rate (%)
89	105.0	3.3
97	38.6	12.3
85	9.2	4.9
86	186.0	5.7
96	15.1	3.2
93	46.0	4.9
92	13.4	3.1
96	0.7	5.5
95	26.2	1.6
94	6.2	7.5
97	3.2	4.9
93	25.4	15.7
96	4.0	13.8
84	6.6	4.3
71	12.7	9.1
76	7.0	9.2
67	5.5	9.6
92	3.2	2.5
85	9.2	0.3
80	2.7	12.9
98	1.3	6.8

Intra-region trade is at its highest level ever. Trade balances are still reasonable. Fiscal discipline has returned to most countries. At the political level, all Latin American governments, even Argentina, have reacted positively to International Monetary Fund (IMF) mandates for economic reform.

Washington may be preoccupied with the Middle East and China, but American businesses are excited about opportunities in the south. Exports from the United States to Latin America, including Mexico, have grown 12 percent over the last five years. Excluding Mexico, exports to other Latin American countries have grown by a whopping 22 percent. This is phenomenal growth considering that several economies have faced fiscal calamity (Argentina), political upheaval (Venezuela and Ecuador), increased drug trafficking (Colombia), and a variety of other disruptive forces. Moreover, trade with Latin America shows no sign of abating. In fact, as **Table 1-2** shows, one-fifth of total U.S. exports to the entire world go to Latin America.

Table 1-2 | Total U.S. Exports to World ($US Billions)

Country	2000	2005	Percent Increase	Year 2005 Percent of Total World Exports
Latin America Ex-Mexico	58	71	22.4	7.8
Mexico	112	120	7.1	13.3
Total Latin America	170	191	12.3	21.1
Canada	176	211	20.0	23.3
Japan	65	55	---	6.1
China	16	41	156.3	4.5
United Kingdom	42	38	---	4.2
Germany	29	34	17.2	3.8
South Korea	28	28	---	3.1
Rest of World	254	306	20.4	33.8
Total U.S. Exports	780	904	15.8	100.0

Source: Office of Trade and Industry, Manufacturing Services, International Trade Administration, U.S. Department of Commerce

Table 1-3 shows U.S. exports to each Latin American country.

Table 1-3 | Total U.S. Exports to Latin America ($US Billions)

Country	2000	2005	Percent Increase (Decrease)
Brazil	15.2	15.3	0.7
Venezuela	5.6	6.4	14.3
Argentina	4.7	4.1	(12.8)
Dominican Republic	4.4	4.7	6.8
Colombia	3.6	5.4	50.0
Chile	3.4	5.2	52.9
Honduras	2.6	3.2	23.1
Costa Rica	2.4	3.6	50.0
Guatemala	1.9	2.8	47.4
El Salvador	1.8	1.8	-0-
Peru	1.7	2.3	35.3
Panama	1.6	2.2	37.5
Jamaica	1.4	1.7	21.4
Trinidad and Tobago	1.1	1.4	27.3
Ecuador	1.0	2.0	100
Uruguay	0.5	0.4	(20)
Paraguay	0.5	0.9	80
Nicaragua	0.4	0.6	50
Bolivia	0.3	0.02	(33.3)
Guyana	0.2	0.2	-0-

Other small countries	3.7	6.6	78.4
Total Latin America Ex-Mexico	58.0	71.0	22.4
Mexico	112.0	120.0	7.1
Total Latin America	170.0	191.0	12.4

Source: USAID: Trade Statistics for Latin America and the Caribbean

As can be seen in **Table 1-3**, nearly 60 percent of 2005 exports went to the top six countries: Brazil, Venezuela, Argentina, the Dominican Republic, Colombia, and Chile. Apparently, several U.S. exporters have reached an understanding with the Venezuelan government to continue significant amount of exports to that country regardless of President Hugo Chavez's anti-American rhetoric.

Relationship Between Washington and Latin America

Historically, the U.S. government and the American people as a group have looked east (Europe) and west (Asia) for international trade, perhaps because immigration to this country came primarily from Europe in the beginning and from Asia later on. Only in the last half-century have Latin American immigrants outnumbered Europeans and Asians. This is perhaps because markets in Europe and Asia have enjoyed significant growth for more than a century, while Latin markets have experienced periodic ups and downs. Perhaps it's because transportation east and west, mainly by boat, was, in the early days, easier than the journey south. Perhaps it's because Europe and, later, Asia offered relatively stable political and economic bases while the political climate throughout Latin America has been anything but stable. Perhaps it's because the economies of Latin America grow and contract like rubber balloons, whereas those of Europe and East Asia are relatively stable.

Whatever the reason, the relationship between Washington and Latin America has been at best rocky and at worst downright antagonistic. Since 1989, various U.S. administrations have made modest attempts to change this relationship. For example, the proposed Free Trade Area of the Americas was an attempt to bring all nations in the Western Hemisphere under a unified trade umbrella. NAFTA continues to bring the economies of the United States, Mexico, and Canada closer to a single standard. Many bilateral trade agreements have been implemented, agreed upon, or are being negotiated. The Dominican Republic-Central American Free Trade Agreement (DR-CAFTA) among the United States, five Central American countries, and the Dominican Republic was implemented in 2004. The U.S.-Chile bilateral Free Trade Agreement also became law in 2004. The United States and Peru then Colombia negotiated free-trade agreements during 2005 and 2006. However, as of this writing, the U.S. Congress has not ratified them.

Without doubt, these trade agreements will benefit both large and small U.S. businesses. Competition with European imports to Latin America is fierce. With free-trade agreements, U.S. companies can effectively compete on price as well as prompt delivery. Strangely, such potential for increased trade with Latin America doesn't seem to have any affect on the U.S. Congress or the administration, regardless of which party is in power. Yes, sometimes a secretary of state travels to one or two Latin American countries. U.S. presidents occasionally make a few obligatory trips. Billions of dollars are poured into Colombia, Bolivia, and Peru to fight the war on drugs. But these efforts go largely unnoticed in the American press. European and Middle Eastern catastrophes, African lawlessness, the rapid economic growth and increased competitiveness of China, outsourcing in India, renewed growth of the Japanese economy—these are today's headlines. From this, it seems obvious that the American public does not have an overriding interest in Latin America, at least not as much as it does in happenings both East and West. This indifference to our southern neighbors influences the direction Washington takes on trade and foreign direct investment, with the government focusing most of its efforts and resources on Europe and Asia.

Fortunately, the business community takes a different tack. As is true in many other matters, American business is three steps ahead of Washington in recognizing the benefits of increased North/South trade and investment. The Summit of the Americas is a good example of the political clout the American business community can muster as a unified front.

Promises of the Summit of the Americas

In December 1994, the first Summit of the Americas was convened in Miami. Heads of state from Canada, the United States, and thirty-one independent Latin American countries met to begin the long process of developing a protocol that would, over time, evolve into the Free Trade Area of the Americas (FTAA). This meeting, the first of several summits to be held in later years, set in motion a process to seek solutions to economic and social problems shared by all the countries in the Western Hemisphere. A second summit was held in Santiago, Chile, in 1998, a third in Quebec City, Canada, in 2001, and a fourth in Mar del Plata, Argentina, in 2005. In addition, a Special Summit of the Americas was held in Monterrey, Mexico, in 2004 to brief eleven new heads of state who had taken office subsequent to the third summit in Quebec City. Between the first and second summits, a 1996 Summit on Sustainable Development was held in Santa Cruz, Bolivia.

At the Quebec City summit in 2001, the thirty-three participating nations agreed that the main goal of the Summit of the Americas process was "to analyze and discuss the challenges that the American continents face in order to seek shared solutions and improve the quality of life of the citizens of the Americas." Participants avowed their "commitment to hemispheric integration and national and collective responsibility for improving the economic well-being and security of our people." That sounds wonderful in the abstract. If it comes to fruition, everyone will benefit. If not, the summits will be just another failed attempt at hemispheric integration.

In addition to these heads-of-state summits, a vast number of intra-hemispheric meetings have been held among lesser representatives of each country to discuss ways to develop uniform standards of customs clearance, protect intellectual property, and safeguard the environment. In addition, judicial conformity, labor standards, and a variety of other matters have been debated. All these meetings, summits as well as lesser gatherings, have been aimed at the inauguration of the FTAA originally scheduled for January 2005. Obviously, this did not occur, mainly because the United States and Brazil could not agree on several items of mutual concern.

If you would like to follow the Summit of the Americas process, its office is located at Summits of the Americas Secretariat, Organization of American States, 1889 F St. NW, Washington, D.C. 20006.

Trade Pact Fever

The Summit of the Americas meetings notwithstanding, the United States has moved forward with many bilateral, and in some case multilateral, trade pacts with Latin countries. As of this writing, trade pacts have been implemented or agreed upon with eleven South and Central American countries and with twenty-four English-speaking Caribbean nations:

1. North American Free Trade Agreement (NAFTA) with Canada and Mexico
2. Dominican Republic-Central American Free Trade Agreement (DR-CAFTA) with the Dominican Republic, Costa Rica, El Salvador, Guatemala, Honduras, and Nicaragua

3. United States-Chile Free Trade Agreement
4. United States-Peru Free Trade Agreement (awaiting U.S. Congressional ratification)
5. United States-Colombia Free Trade Agreement (awaiting U.S. Congressional ratification)
6. United States-Caribbean Basin Trade Partnership Act of 2000, which replaced the expired Caribbean Basin Initiative

In addition, a free trade agreement with Panama is being negotiated, and one with Ecuador is being considered. Uruguay has expressed interest in beginning similar discussions.

Although each trade pact is slightly different, all deal with reducing or eliminating tariffs on goods shipped from Latin America to the United States and on goods shipped from the United States to Latin countries. Some pacts also cover such diverse areas as protection for intellectual property, permission for foreign direct investment, liberalization of customs procedures, and strengthened judiciary practices. NAFTA, of course, is a special case. It covers a multitude of matters especially germane to trade among the United States, Canada, and Mexico, including references to environmental protection and labor practices.

Critics argue that the main effect of free-trade pacts has been to move U.S. jobs to lower-wage countries, thereby depriving American workers of their livelihoods. Certainly, many jobs have moved offshore. But this has made American goods competitively priced with those imported from China, other Asian countries, and Eastern Europe. Nearly all clothing that we wear is now sewn in DR-CAFTA countries. Offshore call centers and backroom financial services in Barbados, Jamaica, and the Dominican Republic pre-dated offshore sourcing in India. Colombian flowers have captured the bulk of the U.S. cut-flowers market. Chilean wine and grapes, Honduran fruit, Ecuadorian seafood, Guatemalan bananas, and many other crops and products from trade-pact members have made major inroads in U.S. markets. Moreover, maquila or export assembly plants of U.S. companies in several Latin nations continue to produce clothing, shoes, and various electronics for shipment back to U.S. markets. It seems abundantly clear that free-trade pacts have in the past and continue now to benefit all Americans, even those whose jobs went south, with lower-priced products needed in everyday life.

Opportunities Abound

Every Latin American nation has benefited from market reforms implemented over the past ten years. While governments are becoming more closely aligned to democratic institutions in the United States and Canada (with a few exceptions), capital continues to flow to the region from the IMF as well as from U.S., Canadian, European, and East Asian governments and the private sector. Business has been legitimatized by new laws governing consumer protection, foreign investments, intellectual-property rights, capital markets, agent/distributor relationships, and a host of other matters necessary to sustain free-market economies. Most important, Latin American consumers in record numbers want to buy American products and services.

A diverse consumer market of more than 550 million people cannot be ignored. Booming commercial and industrial markets that hunger for American technology and management know-how are just too inviting to pass up. The plethora of multilateral and bilateral free-trade agreements that offer U.S. companies a competitive edge over European and Asian rivals are too strategically beneficial to dismiss out of hand. With the fires of global competition destroying cross-border barriers, companies that have waited for the right time to enter or expand in Latin American markets must now move forward.

This is not to say that American business is a stranger to Latin America. On the contrary, U.S. technology, management know-how, goods, and services from a wide range of industries have contributed significantly to the growth of Latin American markets. Moreover, Mexico, Argentina, and Brazil actively solicit foreign trade and investment from American companies. Bilateral trade agreements bring U.S. consumer and industrial products to the stores and factories of Latin America. In fact, doors to Latin America that have previously only been ajar are now swinging wide open.

With some exceptions, I think it's safe to call Latin America a maturing region, no longer destined to be treated as a backwater frontier but rather very close to taking its place with the more economically developed regions of the world. Still, many obstacles to growth remain.

Deficiencies That Still Remain

Although much progress has been made and many external risks are less intrusive today than they were ten years ago, serious problems still lurk in the shadows. Many educational and health-care facilities still lack modern technologies, supplies, and trained staff. Land-line telephone service is still a scarce commodity. Electricity has yet to reach most indigenous populations. Although vastly improved in commercial and industrial centers, roadways, bridges, and ports remain in dismal shape in much of the region. Environmental degradation continues unabated. Social issues have not been properly addressed. Poverty and its evil sister unemployment are huge deterrents to future growth.

Moreover, democracy has yet to win the hearts of most Latin Americans. Asked in a recent poll whether they were satisfied with their country's democratic system, South Americans responded as follows:

- Only 16 percent of those polled in Paraguay said they were satisfied.
- In Peru, a mere 21 percent answered in the affirmative.

- In Brazil, positive responses came from 23 percent of those surveyed.
- In Venezuela, the number was slightly higher at 35 percent.
- In Argentina, which has implemented more economic reforms than any other Latin country, a surprisingly low 42 percent of respondents said they were satisfied with the country's democratic system.

Corruption runs unabated throughout Latin America. Crime turns urban areas into battlefields. Drug trafficking through defenseless smaller countries, as well as through Mexico, poisons a whole generation of young people. Openly hostile military regimes, corrupt and incompetent police and judges, and failing legal systems have caused street crime, kidnappings, and homicides to double and even treble in several Latin capitals. These are very serious problems that must be dealt with quickly and decisively to ease the apprehensions of foreign businesses and travelers.

As newly elected heads of state pick up the reins from their predecessors, one can only hope that they will enhance many of the sound policies already in place, thereby permitting their countries to continue along their current maturation trends. One can only wait and see whether new administrations will revert to previously failed policies, turning back the clock to centralization and protectionism. Unfortunately, we have already seen Venezuela and Bolivia start down this road, and several other nations are precariously balanced on its shoulder.

No one should be misled into thinking that doing business in this vast region is a sure bet. Whether exporting, sourcing with maquila operations, manufacturing or distributing for local markets, or exporting from Latin America to Europe or Asia, doing business in these countries is far more complex than it is in the United States or Canada. Competition from local companies as well as from European and

Asian firms is intense, shipping costs are high, language and dialect barriers are very pronounced, and the business climate in each country is unique. The entire mode of conducting business can be tricky for foreigners, especially Americans. In fact, at times it can seem incomprehensible. (See Chapter 11 for an approach to measuring country risks.)

The more advanced markets in Argentina, Brazil, Chile, Colombia, and Mexico can be especially difficult to master. These countries have well-established business and political protocols, extensive experience with European trade and investment, sophisticated consumers, long-established industrial bases, and well-educated, tough-minded business managers. Moreover, even among these more developed countries, some serious differences confront American businesses.

Intra-regional Cultural and Business Differences

Although many similarities exist among the forty-nine Latin American countries, territories, protectorates, and other entities, several differences should be recognized by any U.S. company contemplating doing business in the region. These differences can be grouped as follows:

Informal underground markets: Brazil, the Dominican Republic, Nicaragua, and Ecuador, and several other countries have thriving and openly available underground markets in goods imported from the United States as well as knock-offs of these products. This tends to destroy the efficiency of distribution systems and disrupts financial systems.

Weakened judicial systems: Although all regional judicial systems have improved markedly over the last decade, some are still fraught with corruption. Judicial corruption is most prevalent in Venezuela, Guatemala, Mexico, and Bolivia.

Environmental degradation: Brazil has the worst history of environmental debasement in the region because of the destruction of the Amazon rain forests by logging companies, farmers, and ranchers. The government has begun to clamp down on the destruction of rain-forest timber, but it has a long way to go to finally put a stop to this desecration.

Crime: Some countries, notably drug-trafficking drop-off countries such as Haiti, Guyana, Mexico, all of Central America and the Dominican Republic, and of course Colombia, have virtually uncontrolled street crime. Murders and robberies are commonplace. Colombia has by far more kidnappings than any other country in the world.

Passive versus aggressive cultures: Ordinary people as well as government officials in Argentina, Colombia, Ecuador, Guatemala, and El Salvador seem to be much more aggressive in their behavior than passive Honduras, Brazil, Chile, and Panama.

Impact of foreign cultures: Europe is the biggest trading partner for Brazil and Argentina. Argentina was settled by immigrants from many Northern and Southern European countries. This European flavor is very evident in Argentina's unique usage of the Spanish language, dress code, and business protocol. Argentina is also by far the most sophisticated of the Latin countries. More than 50 percent of Guyana's population is of East Indian descent. Trinidad is close behind. Most Central Americans are mestizo. Peru has a large population of Japanese.

Such differences are not pronounced in some countries but are very evident in others. Recognizing variations in cultures and market risks is a crucial part of your long-term strategic marketing program. Succeeding chapters will show just how crucial such integration is.

Chapter 2

Latin America's Universal Issues

The world is witnessing a paradox in the making. Latin America is clearly much better off than it was in 1989, the end of the Lost Decade. When all countries in the region (except Cuba, of course) completed the transition from military rule to freely elected civilian governments, enthusiasm for market economies, multiparty elections, free trade, and the privatization of nationalized industries was at its height. But the region was dangerously close to a disastrous implosion created by hyperinflation (four-digit inflation in Brazil), negative growth, unacceptably high unemployment, burdensome foreign debt, and very shaky financial systems. Today, all that has changed. Now Latin America is purring along on all cylinders, making remarkable strides in economic growth and the expansion of private enterprise. The region is without unmanageable inflation, fiscal extravagance, or collapsing judicial systems. Most Latin economies are doing better than they ever have before.

Why then are the politics of the region turning to populism and shifting to the left?

Despite enormous improvements in the availability of consumer goods, electricity distribution and other infrastructure areas, and primary school education, many debilitating issues have not been addressed. The wealth gap continues to widen, especially in countries with large indigenous populations. Health care in rural areas is still abysmal. Air pollution and water contamination are still major health concerns. Sanitary waste disposal remains an elusive concept. Standards of secondary and tertiary education are still well below those of developed countries. With a few exceptions, women are still not treated as equal to men. Although many more Latin Americans can be classified as middle-class and elite than just ten years ago, the working class has not shrunk. Working-class Latinos and Latinas are beginning to rebel. They see their politicians and bosses driving new cars, dressing in designer clothes, and traveling repeatedly to the United States and Europe while they struggle to survive day by day. This working class has already been heard from in Venezuela and Bolivia, throwing out moderate presidents and electing populist left-wing radicals. Ecuador and several Central American nations are on the threshold of moving in the same direction.

Such populism has become a fertile breeding ground for anti-American rhetoric. Venezuelan President Hugo Chavez is especially vocal in his denunciation of the United States, and he has begun to cast his net over all of Latin America. Flush with enormous oil riches, Chavez has embarked on a petro-diplomacy campaign that is already strengthening his grip on the region and turning hearts and minds against the United States. As of this writing, Chavez has done the following:

- Forced big oil into partnerships with his government and charged them exorbitant taxes
- Purchased $1 billion of Argentina's lowly bonds
- Promised to buy Ecuador's and Bolivia's bonds
- Agreed to provide 200,000 barrels of oil per day to Cuba and twelve other Caribbean and Central American nations
- Formed a joint venture with Brazil's Petrobas to build a $2.5 billion refinery near their common border

Chavez even took his campaign directly to the United States, ordering Citgo Petroleum Corp., a wholly owned subsidiary of Petroleos de Venezuela, to sell 12 million gallons of heating oil at prices 40 percent below market price to needy residents of the Bronx and Boston.

There can be little doubt that Chavez has harnessed a growing discontent throughout the region. Little-understood actions by Washington and the dismal failure of democracy to bring relief from social inequities buttress his campaign. Many of my Latino friends express the feeling that democracy has failed and that they are no better off now than they were before 1989 under dictatorial rule and before market economies were instituted. Let us hope that in the near future, the American business community will be influential enough to convince Washington to pay at least as much attention to our southern neighbors as it does to European and Asian countries. Only if America, through its government and business community, provides substantial help to improve Latin America's education, health-care, and judicial systems will the FTAA become a reality. And only with the FTAA or similar trade agreements will American business realize the true potential of trade and investment in Latin America.

Despite Latin America's remarkable economic resilience and the substantial number of market reforms put in place over the last ten years, the lack of attention paid to the resolution of vast inequalities has begun to cause political unrest throughout the region. Many Latin countries blame the United States for shoddy efforts related to reducing poverty, infrastructure deficiencies, health-care shortages, and education weaknesses. The so-called Washington Consensus, which involves reducing the role of the state and implementing economic liberalization of markets, is felt by many to be the single overriding factor that has caused the widening inequality of opportunities for Latin America's working class.

It is certainly easy to blame the behemoth of the North for all of Latin America's ills. But that begs the question. The United States cannot be held responsible for decisions made by duly elected Latin governments. No one forced these governments to adhere to democratic principles. No one coerced them into ignoring their own indigenous peoples. No one goaded them into abrogating their responsibility for rooting out corrupt police and judges. Neither the U.S. government nor the American people had anything to do with the sliding decline of Latin American education and health-care systems. And certainly, no one from the North advocated the widening of the wealth gap so prevalent throughout the region. If anyone is to blame for the mess their social structures are in, it must be Latin Americans themselves. And, with help from the American business community, Latin Americans have the sole responsibility for digging their way out of this morass.

So much for shifts in Latin politics. Let's move on to discuss how competitive each Latin American country really is.

Competitiveness in Latin America

Not every U.S. company with eyes on Latin America has the option of picking which country to focus on. A top executive will have a personal preference, or presumptions will be made about the benefits of specific markets, or a Latin agent will exert undue influence, or a marketing manager will fall for media pronouncements about thriving markets in one country or another. Although any of these reasons may lead to the right choice, increasing competition and changing business environments encourage us to take a more disciplined approach.

The World Economic Forum, an organization that brings together the world's top government and business leaders to discuss the state of the world economy, meets in Davos, Switzerland, once a year. Each year for two decades it has published a competitiveness report comparing the economic, political, and business climates of countries throughout the world. Since 2001, the methodology used in this report has been based on a model developed for the World Economic Forum by noted economists Jeffrey Sachs and John McArthur, called the Growth Competitiveness Index (GCI.) The World Economic Forum's definition of competitiveness is ". . . that collection of factors, policies, and institutions which determine the level of productivity of a country and that, therefore, determine the level of prosperity that can be attained by an economy." The GCI's basic premise is that ". . . a more competitive economy is one that is likely to grow faster over the medium to long-term." If you have a choice about which country to devote resources and energy to, one that ranks at or near the top of the GCI will probably bring the greatest benefits.

The GCI is composed of three separate indexes: the technology index, the macroeconomic environment index, and the public institutions index. The entire list of 117 countries in the 2005 survey is divided into two groups: innovator countries, and all others. Innovator countries are those that have more than fifteen U.S. patents registered per million population. For innovator countries, the GCI rating derives from one-half the technology index plus one-fourth the macroeconomic index plus one-fourth the public institutions index. For all other countries, each sub-index is given an equal one-third weighting.

The technology index consists of several pieces of hard data plus answers to a survey of eleven questions. The hard data are as follows:

- U.S. patents granted per 1 million population
- Gross tertiary school enrollment rate
- Cellular mobile subscribers per 100 inhabitants
- Internet users per 10,000 inhabitants
- Internet hosts per 10,000 inhabitants
- Main telephone lines per 100 inhabitants
- Personal computers per 100 inhabitants

The macroeconomic index survey asks, "Is your country's economy likely to be in a recession next year?" and "Has obtaining credit for your company become easier or more difficult over the past year?" In addition, the index incorporates the following hard data:

- Government surplus/deficit
- National savings rate
- Inflation rate
- Real effective exchange rate
- Lending-borrowing interest-rate spread
- Government debt

The public institutions index consists of a survey of seven questions dealing with judiciary independence, crime, public contracts, financial assets, and bribes paid to public officials. **Table 2-1** shows how each of twenty-one Latin American countries ranked against the 117 countries included in the world index:

Table 2-1 | World Rank 2005 by Competitive Indexes

	Technology Readiness	Macroeconomic Policies	Public Institutions
Chile	50	79	70
Uruguay	63	84	33
Mexico	57	43	71
El Salvador	70	57	54
Colombia	74	61	49
Trinidad/Tobago	62	40	83
Costa Rica	56	82	58
Brazil	50	79	70
Peru	75	70	59
Jamaica	45	99	65
Argentina	59	86	74
Panama	65	74	75

	Technology Readiness	Macroeconomic Policies	Public Institutions
Venezuela	72	75	106
Honduras	95	89	88
Guatemala	96	81	107
Nicaragua	102	110	82
Bolivia	103	84	113
Dominican Republic	67	112	105
Ecuador	100	80	113
Paraguay	111	102	112
Guyana	112	113	109
United States	1	23	18

Source: The Global Competitiveness Report 2005–2006, World Economic Forum, Davos, Switzerland, September 28, 2005

These three indexes are combined to get the Growth Competitiveness Index as shown in **Table 2-2**.

Table 2-2 | Growth Competitiveness Index—Latin America and World Rankings, 2005 and 2004

Note: A score rating of 6 is the most competitive out of 117 countries included in the ranking.

	Score	Rank Latin America 2005	Rank Latin America 2004	Rank World 2005
Chile	4.91	1	1	23
Uruguay	3.93	2	11	54
Mexico	3.92	3	6	55
El Salvador	3.86	4	7	56
Colombia	3.84	5	5	57

Trinidad/Tobago	3.81	6	10	60
Costa Rica	3.72	7	3	64
Brazil	3.69	8	4	65
Peru	3.66	9	12	68
Jamaica	3.64	10	8	70
Argentina	3.56	11	2	72
Panama	3.55	12	9	73
Venezuela	3.22	13	13	89
Honduras	3.18	14	18	93
Guatemala	3.12	15	16	97
Nicaragua	3.08	16	17	99
Bolivia	3.06	17	19	101
Dominican Republic	3.05	18	15	102
Ecuador	3.01	19	14	103
Paraguay	2.80	20	20	113
Guyana	2.73	21	21	115
United States	5.81	N/A	N/A	2

Source: The Global Competitiveness Report 2005–2006, *World Economic Forum, Davos, Switzerland, September 28, 2005*

The purpose of the GCI and its supporting indexes is to alert businesspeople who are thinking about either exporting to Latin America or opening a plant, warehouse, or retail establishment there to the potential benefits and difficulties of choosing one country over another. This is a valuable tool and should be incorporated in your strategic marketing program. This doesn't mean that everyone should choose Chile merely because it is at the top of the ladder. Brazil, El Salvador, or even Guyana might have the type of markets, distribution channels, or competition to make one of those countries a viable choice. But at least with the GCI you have more information with which to make a decision.

It's interesting to note how some of the European and Asian countries compare to Latin America. Since Chile was ranked twenty-third in the world, there must be twenty-two countries ranked higher. The United States ranked second, the five Scandinavian countries, plus Switzerland, Taiwan, and Singapore all ranked ahead of Chile, as did the United Kingdom (ranked 13), Canada (14), and Germany (15). On the other hand, Spain (29), France (30), Thailand (36), China (49), and India (50) all ranked below Chile but above Uruguay (54), Mexico (55), and El Salvador (56). At the other end of the spectrum, only the Kyrgyz Republic and Chad ranked lower than Guyana.

In addition to the GCI, the World Economic Forum publishes an annual Business Competitive Index (BCI). The BCI looks at microeconomic factors to determine sustainable levels of productivity and competitiveness. The underlying concept of the BCI is that ". . . while macroeconomic and institutional factors are critical for national competitiveness, these are necessary but not sufficient factors for creating wealth." The BCI measures two areas for each country:

1. The sophistication of private sector company operations and strategy
2. The quality of the overall national business environment in which companies operate

The BCI is an important adjunct to the GCI in that it is a fairly good measure of what to expect from local businesses in a given country. This will give you a feel as to the amount of resources you will probably have to commit to be successful there. **Table 2-3** shows the BCI ranking for Latin American countries. Note that columns headed "Company Operations and Strategy" and "Quality of National Business Environment" are world rankings for 2005.

Table 2-3 | Business Competitiveness Index: Latin America and World Ranking—2005

Country	BCI Rank Latin America	BCI Rank World	Company Operations and Strategy	Quality of National Business Environment
Chile	1	29	33	29
Brazil	2	49	29	44
Costa Rica	3	50	35	50
Jamaica	4	53	52	53
Colombia	5	56	58	61
El Salvador	6	58	65	65
Mexico	7	60	46	56
Panama	8	61	66	58
Argentina	9	64	68	78
Trinidad/Tobago	10	65	55	62
Uruguay	11	70	80	76
Peru	12	81	77	74
Venezuela	13	92	82	91

Table 2-3 | Business Competitiveness Index: Latin America and World Ranking—2005

Country	BCI Rank Latin America	BCI Rank World	Company Operations and Strategy	Quality of National Business Environment
Dominican Republic	14	101	74	83
Guatemala	15	103	78	90
Honduras	16	105	91	100
Nicaragua	17	106	100	99
Ecuador	18	107	90	95
Guyana	19	110	N/A	N/A
Bolivia	20	113	99	101
Paraguay	21	114	98	96
United States	N/A	1	2	2

Source: The Global Competitiveness Report 2005–2006, World Economic Forum, Davos, Switzerland, September 28, 2005

It seems obvious that, although Chile and Brazil rank 1 and 2 in Latin America, no Latin country offers the competitiveness and hence the ability to create wealth that the United States does. In fact, there are twenty-eight countries ranked ahead of Chile, including the United Kingdom (6), Australia (13), and Canada (15).

Nevertheless, business competitiveness as well as global growth competitiveness are important measures to include in your strategic marketing plans. So are environmental issues.

A Wasting Environment

Many environmental experts believe that the two most serious environmental issues facing Latin America are the following:

- Air and water pollution in urban centers where three-fourths of Latin Americans live
- Depletion and destruction of Amazon rain forests and the related threat to biodiversity

Anyone who has spent time in the megacities of Latin America, such as Mexico City, São Paulo, Santiago, and so on, is well aware of the choking fumes spewed forth from broken-down buses, trucks, and automobiles.

As for the destruction of the Amazon rain forest, that has received an enormous amount of attention in the press over the past two decades. The Brazilian government has tried many times to institute laws to alleviate this destruction. Yet lumbering in the rain forest continues, as does the clearing of land for farms and ranches. Despite cries of anguish from environmentalists, this debasement goes on and on, seemingly without end.

Environmental hazards and degradation are major problems throughout Latin America. With so much turmoil going on for so many years, it's not surprising that the environment has been given short shrift. When people are trying to kill each other with bullets and bombs, the protection of rain forests, mountain streams, and fertile land and the reduction of auto and truck emissions are bound to play second fiddle. Destruction of the rain forest is happening throughout most of Central America, in parts of Mexico, and in huge areas of Brazil, Venezuela, and Colombia. Forests have been destroyed, soil eroded, land poisoned, and water supplies contaminated. There are even signs of climatic shifts occurring because of ecological change.

Some countries are making efforts to improve their environmental assets—Argentina, Chile, Mexico, Brazil, and Costa Rica come to mind. By and large, however, most countries have not yet recognized the severe impact environmental hazards have on economic growth, nor do they understand the relationship between environmental safety and the attractiveness of markets to foreign companies. Here are some dismal statistics from the United Nations Environmental Program:

- During the 1980s, Central America increased agricultural production by 32 percent but doubled its consumption of pesticides.
- A total of 5.8 million hectares of forest cover a year were lost during the first five years of the 1990s.
- Approximately 1,244 vertebrate species are threatened with extinction because of changes in the biodiversity of the rain forest.
- In São Paulo and Rio de Janeiro, air pollution is estimated to cause 4,000 premature deaths a year.
- Waste disposal goes unchecked in the majority of Latin American cities, contaminating water supplies and killing the natural habitat.

Debasement of the environment may have a direct or an indirect impact on your strategic marketing program. For example, it has a direct effect if your products relate to health care. Air pollution and water contamination make people sick, perhaps requiring hospitalization. If you manufacture hospital beds, your market just increased. Environmental degradation might have an indirect effect if your products have wooden components. Laws limiting lumbering in the rain forest might cause prices of hardwood to increase. This could impact the prices you charge for your wooden furniture, even though you don't use rain-forest hardwood. Although environmental hazards and degradation are certainly very serious problems, they don't affect the everyday lives of Latin Americans nearly as much as the constant stream of violence throughout the region.

Violent Crime

The crime rate in Latin America is double the world average, making the region one of the most violent places on earth. More murders occur in Latin America than in any other region of the world, except sub-Sahara Africa. The Inter-American Development Bank estimates that Latin America's GDP per capita would be 25 percent higher if the region's crime rates were only equal to the world average. Violence claims more lives per year than HIV/AIDS and undermines the public's faith in democracy, giving the impression that governments cannot provide public security. Gang violence is especially prevalent in Brazil, Colombia, Jamaica, Central America, and Mexico. Latin American business associations rank crime as the number-one issue holding back increased trade and infrastructure investment.

Various Latin governments have responded to this crime wave with equally horrific methods. As happened when the United States reduced personal freedoms in the name of the war on terrorism, Latin American governments have sacrificed civil liberties in the name of stopping violent crime. Torture is a common weapon used to solicit confessions in Brazil, Mexico, and Peru. Vigilante justice, including lynchings, is increasing in parts of Bolivia, Haiti, Guatemala, and Peru. With violence a part of everyday life, it's easy to understand why so many Latin Americans have lost faith in democratic institutions.

Youth gangs are becoming increasingly violent, primarily in Central America but also in Jamaica, Mexico, Brazil, and

Colombia. Jamaica, known for its high crime rates and murderous youth gangs, saw a 50 percent increase in gang and drug-related murders between 2003 and 2004. The United States has also become an unwitting party to Latin youth gangs. While experts estimate the number of violent gang members in Mexico and Central America at 120,000, they claim the United States harbors at least 700,000 gang members, mostly Latin Americans. The U.S. policy of deporting Latin American criminals after they have served their prison time has given gang members the opportunity to form new gangs in Mexico, El Salvador, Guatemala, Nicaragua, Honduras, and Panama and then, once again, to infiltrate the United States, beginning the cycle anew. Estimates place the number of active gang members in Mexico at 50,000. Total gang members in Central America are estimated at 70,000. The centers of gang activity are still Honduras, El Salvador, and Guatemala, with the highest murder rates in the world. In 2004, the estimated murder rates per 100,000 people were 45.9 in Honduras, 41.2 in El Salvador, and 34.7 in Guatemala. The corresponding figure was 5.7 for the United States. Gangs are reportedly involved in human trafficking, drugs, auto theft, weapons smuggling, and kidnapping.

Now gang violence and narco-trafficking are starting to merge. According to the World Health Organization, narco-gangs use Brazilian children as young as six years old as couriers and lookouts and often pay them with cocaine. Drug addiction among children in Central American and Andean countries has developed into a major problem. U.S. embassies in several countries have found evidence of crack cocaine use and addiction among elementary school children.

According to UN-HABITAT, a large majority of the 30,000 homicides registered annually in Brazil are linked to drug abuse and trafficking. This UN organization estimates that more than 20,000 child and youth couriers, most between ten and sixteen years of age, deliver these drugs. These school-age children often earn more than their parents, giving the kids peer respect and a feeling of importance. This, in turn, feeds their desire to earn even more by trafficking in drugs and other contraband.

Violence is one of the five main causes of death in nearly every Latin American country and is the principal cause of death in Brazil, Colombia, El Salvador, Mexico, and Venezuela. World Vision International claims that the reason Latin America is so violent is that poverty has shut the door on basic human needs, and deep social inequalities plague the region. Among the most marginalized groups are indigenous peoples, Afro-descendants, and women. More than any other group, women bear the brunt of regional violence. Again, according to World Vision International, 30 to 50 percent of women, depending on which country you look at, suffer from psychological violence, and between 10 and 35 percent have suffered physical violence in their own homes. And it isn't just women. Six million children in Latin America are subjected to "severe aggression," meaning they get beat up regularly, and another 80,000 are killed each year while in their homes. Of the top ten countries in the world with the highest child murder rates, Latin America accounts for seven.

A UN report on the state of the world's cities states that Latin America bears the world's highest risk for all types of sex crimes. Approximately 70 percent of reported crimes involve rape, attempted rape, or indecent assault. Mexico, Colombia, and Guatemala report the greatest number of crimes against women.

Does it make sense for any American company to enter Latin American markets as long as these violent criminals operate openly and governments seem unable or unwilling to protect their own citizens? On the surface, the answer seems as if it should be no, with one exception. If you sell law-enforcement products, like handcuffs, police badges, police uniforms, pistols, and so on, then Latin America's violent culture offers thriving markets.

However, it's important to look beneath the surface of Latin America's violence and corruption. When you do, you will see thriving economies, millions of consumers hungry for American-made goods, a wealth of natural resources sorely needed by the world, and many governments trying hard to combat the plethora of social problems. Certainly, it would be unwise to ignore the violence that permeates the region. But by recognizing how and where it occurs and taking safety precautions, American exporters as well as companies that invest in the region will find lucrative markets and willing consumers. In later chapters we'll talk more about strategic marketing and how to integrate matters such as crime, corruption, and other downside factors into your strategic equation and how to maximize profitability in the face of these negatives.

Insidious Corruption

Violence breeds corruption, which breeds violence, which breeds corruption. The two go hand in hand. Latin America not only has its share of violence, it also has its share of corruption. The World Bank estimates that illegal transactions (read corruption) cost the world economy about $1 trillion a year.

I'm certain that every American businessperson has heard of the Foreign Corrupt Practices Act, which prohibits U.S. companies from paying bribes to foreign officials. A new law, the Sarbanes-Oxley Act of 2002, which was enacted to attack accounting fraud (including off-the-books bribes), is a new weapon of the U.S. Department of Justice. All U.S. companies, large or small, must be aware of these laws and have policies on the books to be certain that employees abide by them. Yet in Latin America, bribes are a way of life.

The Foreign Corrupt Practices Act and the Sarbanes-Oxley Act pertain to large bribes or kickbacks given to foreign government officials. Fortunately, the U.S. Congress recognizes the need of American businesses to pay bribes to lower echelon officials and suppliers to remain competitive with in-country companies as well as those from Europe and Asia. These payments are referred to as *grease,* as in *greasing the skids.*

But corruption is more than paying bribes. Transparency International (TI), "a global civil society organization leading the fight against corruption, [which] brings people together in a powerful worldwide coalition to end the devastating impact of corruption on men, women, and children around the world," defines corruption as "the abuse of entrusted power for private gain. It hurts everyone whose life, livelihood, or happiness depends on the integrity of people in a position of authority." Here are some examples of corruption given by TI in the preamble to its 2005 report:

- A father who must do without shoes because his meager wages are used to pay a bribe to get his child into a supposedly free school
- A small shop owner whose weekly bribe paid to the local inspector cuts severely into his modest earnings
- The family trapped for generations in poverty because a corrupt and autocratic leadership has systematically siphoned off a nation's riches
- The prosperous multinational corporation that secured a contract by buying an unfair advantage in a competitive market through illegal kickbacks to corrupt government officials, at the expense of the honest companies who didn't
- Post-disaster donations that never reach the victims because they are diverted to the bank accounts of bureaucrats
- The faulty building, built to lower safety standards because a bribe passed under the table in the construction process, that collapses in an earthquake or hurricane

TI publishes an annual Corruption Perceptions Index, which reflects the opinions of businesspeople and country analysts from around the world. A squeaky-clean score of ten is the best you can do. A score of zero means corruption is rampant. **Table 2-4** shows the results of this survey for the Latin American countries included in the survey.

Table 2-4 | The 2005 Transparency International Corruption Perceptions Index (CPI)

	CPI Score	World Rank
Chile	7.3	21
Uruguay	5.9	32
Costa Rica	4.2	51
El Salvador	4.2	51
Colombia	4.0	55
Trinidad/Tobago	3.8	59
Brazil	3.7	63
Jamaica	3.6	64
Mexico	3.5	66
Panama	3.5	66
Peru	3.5	66
Dominican Republic	3.0	85
Argentina	2.8	98
Honduras	2.6	107
Nicaragua	2.6	107
Bolivia	2.5	117
Ecuador	2.5	117
Guatemala	2.5	117
Guyana	2.5	117
Venezuela	2.3	130
Paraguay	2.1	147

Source: Transparency International, 2005

As can be seen from **Table 2-4**, only Chile and Uruguay had CPI scores above the median of five. Even at that, Chile was way down the world list with a rank of 21 and Uruguay was even farther down at 32. The poor showing of Latin American countries is ample evidence of the level of corruption an American company encounters when entering these markets.

By comparison, the United States had a CPI score of 7.6 and ranked fourteenth in the world. The top five countries with the least corruption were Iceland, with a score of 9.7, Finland (9.6), New Zealand (9.6), Denmark (9.5), and Singapore (9.4). The bottom five, with the most corruption, were Haiti (1.8), Myanmar (1.8), Turkmenistan (1.8), Bangladesh (1.7), and Chad (1.7). The United Kingdom, Canada, and Germany all scored higher than the United States. China (3.2) and India (2.9) were way down the list.

Another report from TI entitled the Global Corruption Barometer 2005 in conjunction with the World Bank Development Indicators tries to express how people feel about the future relative to corruption. The results are about as expected for Latin America:

- More than 50 percent of the survey respondents in Bolivia, Costa Rica, Dominican Republic, Ecuador, Nicaragua, Panama, Paraguay, Peru, and Venezuela believed that corruption has increased a lot.
- Half the respondents in Costa Rica, Ecuador, Mexico, Nicaragua, and Venezuela believed corruption will increase in the next three years.
- In the United States and Germany, 65 percent and 66 percent of respondents, respectively, believe corruption has worsened in the last three years, and 56 percent and 57 percent, respectively, expect this trend to continue.
- In answer to the question, "In the past twelve months, have you or anyone living in your household paid a

bribe in any form?" Thirty-one percent in Paraguay and Mexico answered yes; 30 percent in the Dominican Republic, Ecuador, and Peru answered yes; 11 percent in Guatemala and Bolivia answered yes; and 10 percent in Argentina, Nicaragua, Colombia, Panama, and Venezuela answered yes. Less than 5 percent in Uruguay and the United States answered yes.

• In Bolivia, the Dominican Republic, Guatemala, Mexico, Paraguay, and Peru, about 10 percent of each nation's GDP per capita was paid in bribes.

It goes without saying that corruption is a major problem in Latin America, siphoning off a significant amount of money from the formal economy. It also seems obvious that this is not going to stop any time soon, regardless of laws passed by the U.S. Congress. Now let's turn away from these depressing subjects to the more optimistic world of the Internet and e-commerce.

Selling with E-Commerce

Somewhat surprisingly, online business in Latin America is growing faster than anywhere in the world. Estimates place total e-commerce in the region at approximately $85 billion to $90 billion in 2005. Business-to-business (B2B) e-commerce amounts to about 95 percent of the total. Consumer e-commerce accounts for the rest. Equally surprising is the fact that only a tiny amount of this Internet usage is for retail sales. There are several reasons for this. First, the region's antiquated banking systems constrain the use of credit cards, an important mechanism for paying for Internet purchases. Second, culturally, Latin Americans do not trust the Internet. Third, most of the population prefers to shop in malls where they can see and feel the merchandise. Fourth, only a very small percentage of the region's population can afford a computer with Internet access. And fifth, there aren't very many Internet service providers

(ISPs), hardly any telephone broadband service companies, and only recently the beginnings of a cable market. Surprisingly, several smaller countries, like Guyana, now have cable Internet service that works almost as well as that in the United States.

A very limited number of countries account for most of the Internet usage, although this is rapidly changing as more and more countries get cable. To date, Brazil has 25.9 million Internet users, Mexico has 17 million, and Argentina has 10 million. These three countries account for about two-thirds of the region's Internet users.

Table 2-5 | Internet Users

	Internet Users (Millions)	Population (Millions)	Percent of Population
Chile	6.7	16.1	43
Jamaica	1.1	2.8	39
Argentina	10.0	39.9	25
Costa Rica	1.0	4.1	24
Uruguay	0.7	3.4	21
Trinidad/Tobago	0.2	1.1	18
Mexico	17.0	107.4	16
Peru	4.6	28.3	16
Brazil	25.9	188.1	14
Guyana	0.1	0.8	13
Venezuela	3.0	25.7	12
Colombia	4.7	43.6	10
Panama	0.3	3.1	10
Dominican Republic	0.8	9.2	9

El Salvador	0.6	6.8	9
Guatemala	0.8	12.3	7
Ecuador	0.6	13.5	4
Bolivia	0.3	9.0	3
Honduras	0.2	7.3	3
Paraguay	0.1	6.5	2
Nicaragua	0.1	5.6	2
Canada	20.9	33.1	63
United States	203.8	298.4	68

Source: Internet World Stats; CIA Factbook, 2006

For online sales, the weighting is different. In 2004, Brazil recorded nearly $40 billion in online sales, Mexico had $13.3 billion, and Argentina $6.65 billion. These three countries accounted for 90 percent of all Internet sales.

According to the Infoamericas, Inc., Latin American Market Report of February 2000, the five products accounting for most of the Internet purchases are music, books, PC hardware, airline tickets and hotel reservations, and software. This same report estimates that other products with consumer e-commerce appeal include the following:

- Office equipment and supplies
- Entertainment tickets
- Video games and intelligent toys
- Jewelry
- Wealth management (such as stock brokers, personal bankers, etc.)

Consumer online retailing in Latin America makes a lot of sense, provided your business aims at a very small, elite market. While consumers get a much broader choice of products and services through the Internet, consumer-product companies reduce their advertising costs. The Internet also allows companies to reach a much larger cross-border audience than they could with traditional media.

B2B e-commerce is a different matter entirely. Businesses gain the same advantages in Latin America as they do in the United States: lower costs, smaller inventories, faster billings, and quicker payments. Also, sourcing new bidders is a lot easier and faster on the Internet than trying to do so in-country. According to Forrester Research, e-commerce sales in 2004, both consumer and B2B, by region, were as follows:

- United States $3.2 trillion
- Asia-Pacific $1.6 trillion
- Western Europe $1.5 trillion
- Latin America $82 billion
- Eastern Europe,
  Africa,
  Middle East $68.6 billion

Probably the single most important element in your Latin American market strategy is the future of Internet sales, which, of course, depends on each country's stage of readiness to accept the Internet. This is a difficult factor to measure because each country has its unique configuration of shortcomings, such as the number of telephone lines, dependability of electricity generation, number of ISPs, cable access, banking systems, and so on. However, in July 2002, the Economist Intelligence Unit took a shot at ranking preparedness for e-commence in South America, as shown in **Table 2-6**.

Table 2-6 | South America Internet Preparedness

Note: For comparison purposes, the United States score was 8.41.

Country	Index
Chile	6.36
Mexico	5.67
Brazil	5.31
Argentina	5.14
Venezuela	4.91
Colombia	4.77
Peru	4.43
Ecuador	3.68

Source: The Economist Intelligence Unit, July 2002

Internet usage in Latin America is changing as fast as worldwide technology. Each year will bring radical changes. The only way to accurately include Internet sales in your strategic marketing portfolio is to constantly stay abreast of changes through your in-country representative or partner.

Chapter 3

Latin America's Social Issues

Chapter 2 examined five issues that block Latin America from achieving its full potential by infecting the lives of everyone. This chapter examines an additional six obstacles to growth that I call social issues. These conditions affect specific groups of citizens. The obstacles are the following:

- Education shortfalls
- Gender gap
- Joblessness
- Extreme poverty and the spreading wealth gap
- Broken health-care systems
- Trafficking in persons

As pointed out in earlier chapters, the enigma of Latin America is that while economies continue to grow handsomely, generating increasing income and many new jobs, almost unbearable social conditions go virtually untouched. Yes, several Latin governments have now recognized that they will never join the ranks of rich countries if they cannot resolve their social dilemmas. Some are beginning to take a few tentative steps. By and large, however, they are merely scratching the surface. Inferior education, the subservience of women, extreme poverty, virtually invisible health-care systems, and the most barbarous crime of all, trafficking in persons, persistently plague the region.

Education Shortfalls

While it is true that nearly all school-aged boys and a lesser number of school-aged girls in Latin America now have a primary-school education, the education system is in dire need of restructuring. José Octavio Bordón, an Argentine senator, said at a Canadian Foundation for the Americas conference, "No one disputes that education is vital for economic growth, social advancement, and democracy. Yet most students in Latin America and the Caribbean are deprived of a decent high-quality education." He went on to say, "Enrollment has soared rapidly in the past three decades but quality has eroded just as dramatically; language, math, and science teaching is dismal in most places."

Señor Bordón commented further, "More Latin American students are entering school than ever before, but they don't get very far." A study by the Inter-American Development Bank reveals that only one out of three students enters secondary school, compared with 80 percent in South Korea, Taiwan, and Singapore. Most of those Latin American students never graduate. One-third of all students in Latin America repeat a grade or drop out before completing the sixth grade. One of the main reasons students leave school early is that they need to produce income to support their families. Poverty is so severe that young children are often the only breadwinners in the family. A Washington think tank, the Inter-American Dialogue, issued a report titled *A Program to Promote Educational Reform in Latin America and the Caribbean*. This report points out that on average, the following is true:

- Latin American workers have two years' less schooling than workers in other countries.
- Roughly half the students enrolled in public schools fail the first grade.
- One-third of all students fail in any one year, regardless of the grade they are in.

Overall, educators seem to agree that the heart of the education problem is the very low quality of teaching. People are less educated not only because they leave school early but because the education they do receive is of an inferior quality. The real problem is not lack of access to education but the poor quality of teachers. Teachers' unions in Latin America are very powerful. Yet most of their demands are limited to wages. They seldom, if ever, talk about improving the quality of education.

On average, Latin American countries allocate only 4.5 percent of their GDP to education. Military spending is double or triple that amount. Only Brazil, Costa Rica, Mexico, and Cuba allocate as much as 6 percent of their GDP to education. At the other end of the spectrum, El Salvador, Guatemala, and Peru allocate only 2.5 percent of their GDP to education while spending 20 percent of their budgets on defense.

Unfortunately, boys and girls are not given the same opportunities, even at the primary school level. It is not unusual for girls to be kept home to help with family chores while boys are sent to school. This is an indication of the Latin attitude toward females. Such prejudice is often overlooked in overly zealous marketing plans. However, the antiquated treatment of Latin American women may very well dissuade you from pursuing certain markets. The gender gap remains an eyesore on the facade of Latin business and diminishes the opportunity for market growth.

The Gender Gap

In 2005, the World Economic Forum launched its first-ever survey to measure inequality between women and men in fifty-eight countries. The report of its findings is called Women's Empowerment: Measuring the Global Gender Gap and includes a Gender Gap Index (see **Tables 3-1** and **3-2**). This survey attempts to quantify the size of the gap between men and women in five critical areas:

1. *Economic participation*—equal remuneration for equal work
2. *Economic opportunity*—access to the labor market that is not restricted to low-paid, unskilled jobs
3. *Political empowerment*—representation of women in decision-making positions
4. *Educational attainment*—access to education
5. *Health and well-being*—access to reproductive health care

Of Latin American countries, Costa Rica ranks eighteenth in the world in the composite index but is head and shoulders above everyone else in the region in efforts to narrow the gender gap. It also ranks first in health and well being (resulting from the easy access women have to reproductive health care) and political empowerment (which goes along with the ability of women to hold office at various levels of government.) None of the other countries does well in the world ranking. After Costa Rica, Colombia is the highest, ranked thirtieth in the world. **Table 3-1** shows Latin American gender gap rankings by component. **Table 3-2** shows the world gender gap rankings by component.

Table 3-1 | Gender Gap Index—Latin America Ranking—By Component

	LAC Rank	World Rank	Economic Participation	Economic Opportunity	Political Empowerment	Education Attainment	Health/Well-Being
Costa Rica	1	18	6	6	1	4	1
Colombia	2	30	3	7	2	3	5
Uruguay	3	32	1	4	4	1	8
Argentina	4	35	9	5	3	2	7
Peru	5	47	7	8	5	9	2
Chile	6	48	8	2	7	7	3
Venezuela	7	49	2	1	8	6	9
Brazil	8	51	4	3	9	5	6
Mexico	9	52	5	9	6	8	4

Source: Women's Empowerment: Measuring the Global Gender Gap, World Economic Forum, May 16, 2005

Table 3-2 | Gender Gap Index—World Ranking—By Component

	World Rank	Economic Participation	Economic Opportunity	Political Empowerment	Education Attainment	Health/Well-Being
United States	17	19	46	19	8	42
Costa Rica	18	49	30	9	14	30
Colombia	30	41	38	15	13	52
Uruguay	32	36	26	36	2	56
Argentina	35	55	29	26	3	54
Peru	47	50	44	38	47	31
Chile	48	52	20	44	40	45
Venezuela	49	38	13	52	33	58
Brazil	51	46	21	57	27	53
Mexico	52	47	45	41	44	51

Source: Women's Empowerment: Measuring the Global Gender Gap, World Economic Forum, May 16, 2005

This is a very revealing survey, and it points out one of the more serious cultural differences that Americans must deal with. Here in the United States, the feminist movement of the 1970s opened the door of opportunity for women in the business world. Although the number of women rising to top positions is still abysmally low, the mere fact that this country now has seen several female CEOs of major corporations indicates that women are beginning to crack the glass ceiling. Similar changes are happening on the political scene. More and more women are being elected to local, state, and federal office. In fact, more than one-third of several state legislatures are comprised of women.

But such empowerment of women has not happened in Latin America. With the possible exception of Costa Rica, Colombia, and recently Chile, Latinas are not offered the same opportunities as their male counterparts in either the workplace or the political sphere. Unfortunately, as discussed in Chapter 5, this unequal treatment of women is a basic part of the Latin culture. To overcome this gender gap, cultural changes to reflect an entirely different way of regarding women and their capabilities in the business and political spheres must occur. We could certainly help our Latin American neighbors by letting them see that America women play crucial roles in every aspect of the business community. By observing how well American women deal with complex business issues, perhaps Latinos will eventually close this nefarious gender gap. Here are a few interesting points that **Tables 3-1** and **3-2** do not reveal:

- The top five countries in the Gender Gap Index were Scandinavian countries
- Canada (7) ranked higher than Western European countries and the United States
- The United Kingdom (8), Germany (9), and France (13) all ranked higher than the United States

- The two lowest ranked countries in the survey were Turkey (57) and Egypt (58)
- China (33) ranked below Costa Rica but above the rest of Latin America
- India (53) ranked sixth from the bottom in the survey

The Evils of Joblessness

Almost as disheartening to the American business community as the gender gap is the near hopelessness of Latin American workers who cannot or will not find jobs. Despite enormous debt write-offs by rich-country governments and banks, a plethora of foreign direct investment, the abolition of runaway inflation, and the stabilization of capital markets and banking systems, unemployment continues at unacceptable levels throughout the region, except in Mexico. The UN Economic Commission on Latin America and the Caribbean judges that unemployment throughout the region has jumped 10 percent in the last ten years. Some countries, notably Argentina and Venezuela of the major economies and Honduras and the Dominican Republic of the minor ones, have seen unemployment rates accelerate even more.

Argentina, which in the early 1990s was considered the most advanced and rapidly growing economy in the region, now suffers unemployment of more than 11 percent. Children roam the streets of Buenos Aires looking for handouts, trying to earn a few pesos for bread. More than 1.5 million children under the age of fifteen work full time. Of course, most of them work in the informal or underground economy, which evades formal government measurement.

In Colombia, with a reported unemployment rate of 10.2 percent, one out of five children from the age of five to seventeen is forced to work, mostly in the informal economy, to support the family. Although the minimum wage in Colombia is the equivalent of $41 per month, close to 2.5 million Colombian children toil for less than this. No one knows how much kids earn in the informal economy.

Brazil, with many flourishing industries, reports an overall unemployment rate of nearly 10 percent. In major urban centers such as São Paulo, Belo Horizonte, and Rio de Janeiro, however, at least 25 percent of able adults are out of work. Children looking for work are not counted. Illiteracy prevents at least 15 percent of the nation's population from getting work. Meanwhile, the crime rate in these same urban centers continues its never-ending rise.

These are dismal statistics. While professionals, government bureaucrats, and many business owners and executives drive Mercedes and vacation in Miami or Paris, most of the working class of the region swelters in pitiable poverty. As you begin to do business in Latin America, you will soon be asking yourself how businesses can flourish while such a large group of adults and children live in poverty.

This inequity in wealth is beginning to change the composition of governments throughout the region. Politicians who promise more jobs and less poverty are winning election after election. Venezuelans elected Hugo Chavez as President; Bolivians elected Evo Morales; Argentines elected Nestor Kirchner; and Brazilians elected Luiz Inacio Lula de Silva. Chileans, Ecuadorians, Peruvians, and citizens of many Central American and Caribbean countries will be going to the polls to elect new presidents. Will they be equally left-leaning populists? Possibly. Why should that be? Why, when the economies of most Latin American countries are humming along and local businesses are doing better than they have for decades? Why would the citizens of these countries turn away from the very market reforms that have brought their countries out of the doldrums?

For one simple reason: Wealth has not trickled down to the populace in general. Too many people are worse off now than they were under pre-1990s dictators. Huge indigenous populations live in squalor. Persistent extreme poverty, a huge gap between rich and poor, and above all, joblessness, are taking their toll.

Table 3-3 shows how severe the jobless problem in several Latin American countries really is. Honduras is the worst, with an unemployment rate of 28 percent. Although doing much better than Honduras, the Dominican Republic (17 percent), Paraguay (16 percent), Uruguay (12.5 percent), Venezuela (12.3 percent), and Jamaica (11.5 percent) have enough joblessness to cause great concern among potential American exporters. No one likes to see riots in the streets. Yet roadblocks that bring transportation and commerce to a halt are the only means poor out-of-work Latinos have of expressing their anger.

Table 3-3 | Unemployment Rates, 2005

Country	Unemployment Rate (Percent)	Population Below Poverty Line (Percent) **
Mexico	3.6	40
El Salvador	6.5	35
Costa Rica	6.6	18
Nicaragua	6.9	50
Guatemala	7.5	75
Bolivia	8.0	64
Trinidad/Tobago	8.0	21
Chile	8.0	18
Peru	8.7	54
Panama	8.7	37
Guyana	9.1	N/A
Ecuador	9.7	52
Brazil	9.9	22
Colombia	10.2	49

Argentina	11.1	38
Jamaica	11.5	19
Venezuela	12.3	47
Uruguay	12.5	22
Paraguay	16.0	32
Dominican Republic	17.0	25
Honduras	28.0	53
Canada	6.8	16
United States	5.1	12

** Definitions of poverty line are unique to each country
Source: Various in-country agencies; CIA Factbook, 2005; U.S. Commercial Service, Department of State

The angst Latin Americans feel was adequately expressed in a recent poll by Los Medios de Latinoamérica. It showed that 75 percent of respondents between the ages of twelve and sixty-four answered yes to the question, "I am worried that I (or a family member) will lose his or her job and not find another one." The breakdown by country was Argentina (85 percent), Brazil (79 percent), Venezuela (79 percent), Mexico (76 percent), Chile (72 percent), and Colombia (71 percent.) Fifty-five percent of the rest of South American respondents answered yes to the question. Of the total responses from Central America and the Caribbean, 75 percent said they were worried. Clearly, with such a high percentage of Latin Americans worried about their jobs, there is very little time or energy left to appreciate market reforms or democracy.

So far we have discussed only the official rate of unemployment prepared by the each country's government. But this ignores a very large segment of the Latin American population, those people engaged in the informal or underground economy. This economy includes street vendors, children, domestic help, illegal activities such as illicit drug pushing, bribes and kickbacks, and a variety of other activities that generate income but defy measurement by the government.

In some countries the informal economy generates as much or more income than the formal economy. Felipe Larrain Bascunan, professor of economics at Catholic University of Chile, estimates that the income generated by the informal economy in Chile is equal to 19 percent of GDP, and in Bolivia, it is as much as 67 percent of GDP. This represents an enormous amount of effort, time, and skill and causes a very large distortion in the official statistics. Unfortunately, as long as the official rate of unemployment remains high, an increasing number of people will look to the informal economy for their income.

It goes without saying that with these high rates of official unemployment coupled with gross uncertainties in the informal economy, a great many working age people will, of necessity, live below the poverty line, and more than a few will live in extreme poverty.

Extreme Poverty and the Spreading Wealth Gap

Various analysts place the number of Latin Americans who are poor at between 200 million and 250 million. That's about 40 percent of the entire population of the region. Moreover, these same regional experts claim that about 93 million, nearly 50 percent of the region's poor people, or about 17 percent of Latin America's entire population, live in extreme poverty. The UN's definition of extreme poverty is income of less than one U.S. dollar per day

Of all the shortcomings of Latin America, this very high level of poverty is the most pervasive factor keeping citizens from reaping the benefits of market economies. As long as people are oppressed by poverty, nothing is as important to them as surviving another day with bread on the table.

Table 3-4 shows each country's percent of population who live in extreme poverty, that is, who live on less than $1 per day.

Table 3-4 | Percent of Population Living in Extreme Poverty

	Rank	Population (Millions)	Percent Living in Extreme Poverty	Population Living in Extreme Poverty (Millions)
Uruguay	1	3.2	2.5	0.1
Chile	2	15.1	4.7	0.7
Costa Rica	3	4.0	8.2	0.3
Mexico	4	105.0	12.6	13.2
Brazil	5	186.0	13.2	24.6
Panama	6	3.2	17.4	0.6
Ecuador	7	13.4	19.4	2.6
Dominican Republic	8	9.2	20.3	1.9
Argentina	9	38.6	20.9	8.1
El Salvador	10	6.6	22.1	2.6
Venezuela	11	25.4	22.2	5.6
Colombia	12	46.0	23.7	10.9
Peru	13	26.2	24.4	6.4
Guatemala	14	12.7	30.9	3.9
Paraguay	15	6.2	33.2	2.1
Bolivia	16	9.2	37.1	3.4
Nicaragua	17	5.5	42.4	2.3
Honduras	18	7.0	54.4	3.8

Note: Guyana, Jamaica, Trinidad and Tobago, and other small Caribbean countries were excluded from this survey.

Source: The Millennium Development Goals: A Latin America and Caribbean Perspective, UN Economic Commission on Latin America and the Caribbean

As shown in **Table 3-4**, the five countries with the lowest poverty rates—that is, those countries that have the lowest percentage of their populations living below that country's extreme poverty line—are Uruguay, Chile, Costa Rica, Mexico, and Brazil, in that order. These countries should have no difficulty reaching the United Nations Millennium Development Goals (MDGs) of halving their poverty rates by 2015. The Chilean government has already done remarkably well, causing that country's poverty rate to drop from 38 percent of the population in 1990 to 18.8 percent in 2005. Over the same period, extreme poverty rates fell from 12.9 percent to 4.7 percent.

A second group of countries, where large segments of the population continue to live in extreme poverty, have not done as well. This intermediate group of nations includes Panama, Ecuador, the Dominican Republic, Argentina, El Salvador, Venezuela, Colombia, and Peru, descending in that order. According to the Millennium Goals study, to halve their poverty rates by 2015, each of these countries needs to raise its GDP per capita 3.1 percent per year.

According to the Human Development Report issued by the United Nations Development Program, Brazil has the most unequal distribution of wealth of any country in the world. If only 5 percent of the wealth of the richest 20 percent of the population were transferred to the poorest 20 percent of the population, the overall poverty rate would be reduced from 22 percent to 7 percent. That translates to 26 million Brazilians lifted out of poverty.

The five countries with the worst poverty levels are Guatemala (with about 31 percent of its population living in extreme poverty), Paraguay (33 percent), Bolivia (37 percent), Nicaragua (42 percent), and Honduras (54 percent). To reach the UN's goal by 2015, each of these nations needs to raise its GDP per capita by 4.4 percent per year. Perhaps I am a bit pessimistic, but increasing GDP per capita by 4.4 percent per year is equivalent to a 6.7 percent annual growth rate for the entire country. To expect this big an improvement in such a short period of time seems outlandish. I suspect that more harm than good would come from policies enacted to meet this goal, quite likely driving even more people into abject poverty.

The United Nations Population Fund claims that "poverty and inequity continue to be key issues in Latin America and the Caribbean. The region faces the greatest socioeconomic inequalities in the world, and changes in the distribution of income during the period 1990–2004 have been minimal." That says it all.

While these statistics paint a dismal picture, all is not lost. Many Latin American governments have, in fact, begun a wide range of social programs designed to ameliorate the uneven distribution of wealth. Here are a few examples:

- Brazil launched a family grant program that pays families 95 reals a month (about $40) to keep their children in school. Another effort, the Zero Hunger program, gives families additional reals to buy groceries.
- Argentina also started a program to pay families a monthly stipend to keep children in school. Moreover, the Argentine government pays a monthly subsidy of 150 pesos (about $52) to unemployed heads of household.
- Chile set up a program to offer 180,000 families employment rather than financial assistance.
- Venezuela began several programs aimed at alleviating poverty. For example, more than half the population now purchases food at subsidized prices; the school population increased by nearly 4 million students, many of whom were granted scholarships; and 15,000 Cuban doctors brought medical care to both rural and urban areas.

Certainly these programs help to alleviate poverty. However, they don't always reach the indigenous peoples who are, in fact, the poorest. In some countries, indigenous peoples account for an enormous slice of the population. They seldom have schools in their villages. Health-care professionals are unknown to them. Mothers seldom, if ever, receive reproductive care. Food is grown and hunted, not purchased in stores. Here are some findings of a World Bank study, *Indigenous Peoples, Poverty, and Human Development: 1994–2004*:

- During the 1990s, the indigenous poverty gap deepened, and the number of indigenous peoples living in extreme poverty shrank more slowly than ever before.
- Being indigenous increases an individual's probability of being poor, and this was as true at the end of the decade as at the beginning.
- Indigenous peoples continue to have fewer years of education, and the quality of education they do receive is worse.
- Indigenous peoples, and especially women and children, have less access to basic health care.

Until solutions can be found to bring indigenous peoples into the twenty-first century, no government programs are going to be successful in lifting them out of extreme poverty. This situation is analogous to the living standards of large groups of Native Americans. To this day, many Native Americans continue to live in extreme poverty on reservations with decrepit housing and no professional health care or schools, especially in the Dakotas and Wisconsin.

Table 3-5 shows a breakdown by country of indigenous populations.

Table 3-5 | Indigenous Peoples of Latin America (Estimate in Millions)

	Total Population	Indigenous Population	Percent of Total Population
Bolivia	9.2	5.1	55.0
Peru	26.2	11.8	45.0
Guatemala	12.7	5.5	43.0
Mexico	105.0	31.5	30.0
Ecuador	13.4	3.4	25.0
Guyana	0.7	0.1	7.0
Honduras	7.0	0.5	7.0
Panama	3.2	0.2	6.0
Nicaragua	5.5	0.3	5.0
Paraguay	6.2	0.3	5.0
Colombia	46.0	1.8	4.0
Chile	15.1	0.4	3.0
Argentina	38.6	1.2	3.0
Venezuela	25.4	0.5	2.0
El Salvador	6.6	0.6	1.0
Jamaica	2.7	0.1	1.0
Trinidad/Tobago	1.1	0.1	1.0
Costa Rica	4.0	0.1	1.0
Brazil	186.0	0.9	0.5
Uruguay	3.2	0	0
Canada	32.8	0.7	2.0
United States	295.7	2.6	0.9

Source: United Nations Economic Commission on Latin America and the Caribbean; U.S. Commercial Service, U.S. Department of State; in-country sources

Except for dealing with indigenous peoples, Latin governments have made strides in alleviating poverty. Surely, if governments across the board began redistributing some of their newfound wealth, especially in countries like Mexico, Venezuela, and Ecuador, which have benefited from windfall oil prices, the region would eventually work its way out of the disastrous poverty dilemma that has torn it apart for so many years.

Broken Health-Care Systems

The World Health Report 2005 has predicted that each year, 11 million children under the age of five years will die from largely preventable causes, mostly HIV/AIDS. Among these children will be 4 million babies dying in the first month of life. More than 500,000 women will die in pregnancy, childbirth, or shortly thereafter. Yes, those statistics relate to the world and yes, we all know that Africa has more cases of HIV/AIDS than any other region. However, Latin America is right behind Africa and gaining ground.

Second only to crime and violence, a broken health-care system is the most insidious barrier holding Latin America back. Health care throughout the region is abominable. The lack of adequate reproductive care for women and the lack of any meaningful effort to fight HIV/AIDS are two of the most destructive parts of the system.

As can be seen in **Table 3-6**, nearly 3.3 million Latin Americans are infected with HIV/AIDS. In 2005 alone, about 300,000 new cases were reported and more than 130,000 people died from AIDS. The Caribbean is the second most-infected area in the world, surpassed only by sub-Sahara Africa. Haiti is the worst in all of Latin America, with 5.6 percent of the population infected. Although HIV is transmitted primarily heterosexually, Central America and mainly the Caribbean have large, though hidden, homosexual populations. In contrast, HIV/AIDS in South America is transmitted primarily through drug use, according to HIV InSite of the University of California San Francisco School of Medicine.

Table 3-6 | Latin Americans Living with HIV/AIDS

	Number of People with HIV/AIDS (Thousands)	Population (Thousands)	Percentage of Population with HIV/AIDS
Brazil	1,302	186,000	0.7
Colombia	322	46,000	0.7
Mexico	312	105,000	0.3
Argentina	270	38,600	0.7
Venezuela	178	25,400	0.7
Dominican Republic	156	9,200	1.7
Peru	131	26,200	0.5
Guatemala	140	12,700	1.1
Honduras	126	7,000	1.8
El Salvador	46	6,600	0.7
Trinidad/Tobago	42	1,300	3.2
Chile	45	15,100	0.3
Jamaica	32	2,700	1.2
Ecuador	40	13,400	0.3
Panama	29	3,200	0.9
Paraguay	31	6,200	0.5
Costa Rica	24	4,000	0.6
Guyana	18	700	2.5
Nicaragua	11	5,500	0.2
Uruguay	9	3,200	0.3
Bolivia	9	9,200	0.1
United States	1,782	300,000	0.6

Source: World Health Organization; CIA Factbook; World Vision International; HIV Insite; FN–Country Reports

HIV/AIDS isn't the only health issue holding Latin America back. Throughout the region, health care for all but the elite class is well below the standards of the developed world. Health insurance is seldom available. Reproductive care for women is nonexistent among the poor and indigenous peoples. *The World Health Report 2000*, released by the World Health Organization, found that the main reasons for the failings of these health care systems are the following:

- Many government health programs focus on the public sector, disregarding the private sector.
- In many countries, physicians work simultaneously for the public sector and private practice. This means the public sector subsidizes private practice.
- There is a strong black market in health care, both in pharmaceuticals and in physician care. Widespread corruption, bribery, moonlighting, and other illegal practices flourish.
- Health ministries tend not to enforce regulations.

The World Health Organization's report also ranks all countries of the world according to how well their health-care systems are functioning. **Table 3-7** shows the somewhat surprising results.

Table 3-7 | Latin America's and World's Health Systems Rankings

	Latin America	World
Colombia	1	22
Chile	2	33
Costa Rica	3	36
Dominican Republic	4	51
Jamaica	5	53
Venezuela	6	54

Paraguay	7	57
Mexico	8	61
Uruguay	9	65
Trinidad/Tobago	10	67
Nicaragua	11	71
Argentina	12	75
Guatemala	13	78
Panama	14	95
Ecuador	15	111
El Salvador	16	115
Brazil	17	125
Bolivia	18	126
Guyana	19	128
Honduras	20	131

Note: 190 countries took part in the study.
Source: World Health Organization: World Health Report 2000

Also, although the world average cost for private health care is about 25 percent of household income (except in the United States, where it can range up to more than 50 percent), in most sections of Latin America it is not uncommon for families to pay nearly 100 percent of their income for health care. This of course, is why so many families treat themselves instead of using a physician. This in turn increases the death rate for many diseases. All in all, health care throughout Latin America is another social inequity that prevents the region from attaining its rightful place in the world's economic spectrum.

To conclude this discussion of debilitating social issues, let's take a look at what must be one of the world's most destructive, evil, and barbarous crimes—trafficking in persons.

Trafficking in Persons

During 2000, the U.S. Congress passed a law called the Trafficking and Violence Protection Act, the main purpose of which was to report on the worldwide epidemic of trafficking in persons for sexual purposes, forced labor, or any other activity that compels a person to perform a deed contrary to that person's wishes. Originally, trafficking statistics were confined to the cross-border movement of persons. Now, in-country trafficking is also included.

For most Americans, trafficking in persons means Chinese stowaways aboard freighters or Latinos smuggled across the Rio Grande. But to the rest of the world it means much more.

The U.S. State Department undertakes to analyze trafficking from information gathered at its embassies around the world. These studies reveal the appalling fact that slave labor and involuntary servitude are as common as sexual exploitation.

The fifth annual Trafficking in Persons Report assigns each country to one of four tiers:

1. **Tier 1:** Countries whose governments fully comply with the act's minimum standards
2. **Tier 2:** Countries whose governments do not fully comply with the act's minimum standards but are making significant efforts to bring themselves into compliance with those standards
3. **Tier 2A**—Special Watch List: Countries whose governments do not fully comply with the act's minimum standards but are making significant efforts to bring themselves into compliance with those standards, and
   - The absolute number of victims of severe forms of trafficking is very significant or is significantly increasing.
   - There is a failure to provide evidence of increasing efforts to combat severe forms of trafficking in persons from the previous years.
   - The determination that a country is making significant efforts to bring itself into compliance with min-

imum standards is based on commitments by that country to take additional steps over the next year.

4. **Tier 3:** Countries whose governments do not fully comply with the minimum standards and are not making significant efforts to do so.

Obviously, Tier 3 countries are the worst offenders. The governments of these countries aren't even trying to stop trafficking. In the past, Venezuela, Belize, Bolivia, Ecuador, Jamaica, and Cuba fell into Tier 3. Thanks to pressure from the United States, by 2006 the only Latin American nations still classified as Tier 3 countries were Venezuela, Belize, and Cuba. That puts these countries in a league with the ten other Tier 3 countries worldwide: Iran, Laos, North Korea, Saudi Arabia, Sudan, Syria, Uzbekistan, and Zimbabwe. Membership in that group is not something to be proud of. Hopefully, in the near future Venezuela and Belize, at least, will undertake procedures to stop the horrific practice of trafficking in persons. Let's take a look at what the U.S. State Department report has to say about Venezuela.

The report defines Venezuela as a source, transit, and destination country for women and children trafficked for purposes of sexual exploitation. Women and children from Colombia, China, Peru, Ecuador, and the Dominican Republic are trafficked to and through Venezuela. Venezuelans are trafficked internally for sexual exploitation, usually from rural to urban areas, then on to Western Europe (particularly Spain and the Netherlands), Mexico, Aruba, and the Dominican Republic. Children living near the Venezuelan border are trafficked to the mining camps of Guyana, where they are sexually exploited, or to Colombia, where they are forced to join armed insurgent groups. Venezuela is also a transit point for illegal immigrants from China.

Although the Venezuelan government has begun to take minimal actions against trafficking in persons, no arrests, prosecutions, or convictions have been made. During 2005, the government did launch a national campaign to educate the public about the dangers of trafficking, using posters and radio and television spots. However, the penalties for anyone convicted of this act are so small that they do nothing to deter or stop the practice.

In addition to the Tier 3 group, the Latin American Tier 2 Watch List for 2006 was comprised of Argentina, Bolivia, Brazil, Jamaica, Mexico, and Peru.

Summary

The eleven social issues discussed in this chapter and the universal issues discussed in the previous chapter point to the long road Latin America must travel to reach developed-nation status. Like less-developed regions of Africa and to a lesser extent Asia, Latin America's extensive background of political upheaval has prevented it from making much progress in the very difficult task of dealing with these issues. Unlike much of Africa, however, Latin America has at least evolved democratically elected governments. Eventually, one would hope, these governments will obtain the resources and the will to seriously address their nations' social deficiencies. Fortunately, the battle has already been joined in several countries. Chile, Costa Rica, and Argentina, for instance, have made substantial progress in improving their education systems. Brazil continues to inch toward the prevention of further destruction of its rain forests. Mexico, prodded by NAFTA, has grudgingly begun to recognize what has to be done to integrate the indigenous peoples of the south into Mexican society. Trinidad and Tobago, while continuing the struggle to permanently stabilize its government, is using some of its newfound wealth to alleviate island poverty.

As long as the economies of Latin America continue improving as they have in the past ten years, eventually the region will throw off many of these nefarious shortcomings and gain entrance to the developed world of the twenty-first century. If the American business community continues to support these efforts, the time it takes Latin countries to reach this plateau will be measurably shortened.

Chapter 4

Major Market Opportunities

Argentina's debt default, Venezuela's flirtation with a duly elected dictator, Bolivia's nationalization of its natural gas industry, Ecuador's currency failure, and shifts to the left in virtually all South American nations took the wind out of the sails of many U.S. companies who had thought that emerging Latin markets, and especially those of South America, were ripe for the taking. All those companies had to do was bring their products to market or build a manufacturing plant, and returns would far exceed those possible in Europe, China, Canada, or at home. The rewards from burgeoning market demand and strengthening economies have, indeed, brought many new foreign entrants to Latin America. But since the new millennium, a number of startling events have taught a valuable lesson. The risks of doing business throughout the region are far greater than had previously been thought. The reaction of several South American governments to the failed experiments with democracy has generated a more sobering, realistic view of business opportunities in all of Latin America.

Although all Latin governments have made progress with their macroeconomic reforms, not one has addressed the counter-problems such reforms bring in the social sphere. In fact, poverty levels and income inequalities are becoming more pronounced year by year. Nor have the leaders of Latin America come to grips with political institutions ill equipped to deal with democracy. And, despite economic reforms, the majority of the region's exports, other than traditional agricultural and mining commodities and a limited

71

number of manufactured goods from Brazil, remain non-competitive in world markets.

All Latin American leaders must work rapidly toward developing genuine democratic regimes so that elections will be fair and free of fraud, and citizens will feel secure in voting for candidates of their choice. They must also spend a significant amount of political capital and financial resources resolving social inequalities. But the biggest challenge of all will be to design institutions that solidify economic reforms already implemented and allow social reforms to progress unfettered. Boards of public health and education, anti-trust agencies, health-care distributors, impartial judiciaries, honest law enforcement, and effective tax collection bureaus, among many other institutions, must be put in place, and soon, to prevent the region's social ills from causing massive backsliding in economic and political reforms.

With all this in mind, it should be obvious that doing business in any Latin American country is never easy. It can be a frustrating experience, fraught with potential disaster. It's very easy to feel that you are being pushed to the edge. Although all countries proclaim a willingness, even an eagerness, for U.S. investment and trade, the external market risks facing any foreign company, whether exporting, sourcing, or operating an offshore facility, can be overwhelming. The American business community will face far greater challenges in Latin America than in Europe or Asia.

Governments are more involved in everyday life. In many countries the military is visibly active. Infrastructures are depleted. Ports are crowded. Overland transport in less-developed countries is abominable. And citizens are more reluctant to accept foreigners. In fact, it's fair to say that the entire mode of doing business in this region is averse to traditional American marketing, production, and personnel policies. Moreover, as I continue to stress, to succeed anywhere in Latin America, you must plan for the long haul. There is no quick fix here. You will have to feel your way through the maze of market and cultural anomalies that at times seem bent on turning you back.

Yet U.S. companies that have ventured into Latin America have been richly rewarded. The potential for huge returns on investment is there. The possibilities for double-digit growth in earnings are enormous. If you have the courage to tackle the difficult but not unmanageable external market forces, I guarantee you won't be sorry for trying Latin America, and especially South America.

Varied Market Strategies

It's a mistake to view Latin America as a single market. Forty-nine separate countries, territories, departments, commonwealths, and protectorates with more than 550 million people who speak hundreds of dialects, originating from Spanish, Portuguese, French, German, Dutch, Italian, Creole, and native Amerindian tongues, make this region anything but homogeneous. Differences in economic development, social conditions, political environments, and a variety of other factors mean that you must devise separate strategic marketing plans for each country you intend to do business in. This is true whether you plan to restrict your efforts to exporting alone or you plan to invest in plants, distribution centers, or customer-service facilities. Certainly, the magnitude of the obstacles to be overcome can be daunting. However, with detailed planning and preparation, there is no reason why you cannot succeed.

Economically, politically, historically, and especially in relation to the United States, Central American nations differ markedly from South American countries. Central America is like a child growing up, a child who depends on the guidance, protection, and financial support of parents and has a hard time leaving the nest when it's time to confront the world as an adult. The real mother country, Spain, had long since abandoned her offspring when the United States stepped in to become a foster parent. Now, with the

United States more interested in fighting Middle East wars and solving domestic problems than in sustaining Central American governments that do not seem very grateful to begin with, these seven countries are struggling to adapt to a new world of self-sufficiency.

Over the past 400 years, Central America has been alternately conquered by foreign mercenaries, exploited by foreign companies, occupied by foreign troops, decimated by civil wars funded by foreigners, courted by foreign governments, and pounded by hurricanes, droughts, earthquakes, and volcanic eruptions. During recent times, Central America has become a major stopover for illicit drugs on their way from South America to U.S. markets, a training ground for CIA agents, and the battleground for U.S. efforts to halt the spread of communism in the Western Hemisphere. From the 1520s, when Spanish conquistadores invaded this out-of-the-way stretch of land in search of gold to the present, Central America has been fraught with turmoil. Nevertheless, this region does offer some attractive features:

- It is the only land link between North America and South America.
- It is the easiest and fastest way to move goods and people between the Atlantic and Pacific Oceans, either through the Panama Canal or overland across stretches of land that range from 30 to 300 miles.
- It has an abundance of untapped natural resources, such as agricultural products, timber, sea life, and minerals.
- It has a small but eager population of semi-skilled and unskilled workers, hungry for jobs.

Military aggression has been muted. All countries now have elected governments. A growing number of people realize that political violence does not offer a permanent solution to their problems. Citizenries are beginning to see that the only sustainable way out is to negotiate settlements with rebel bands, to strengthen their political, financial, and social institutions, and to let the free market stabilize prices.

Central America has begun the painful process of moving from the war-torn 1980s and the economically depressed 1990s to the modern day, enacting legislation that governments hope will permit these nations to move with the rest of the hemisphere into the twenty-first century. Dramatic steps are being taken toward free trade and market liberalization. By 2015, DR-CAFTA will have eliminated or greatly reduced tariffs on almost all products. Many protectionist measures that had previously hampered trade throughout the region have already been reduced or eliminated, enhancing opportunities for intra-region trade. Efforts are currently being made to modify complex rules governing exchange controls, multiple exchange rates, and restrictions on capital repatriation. As a means to attract foreign investment, countries are now offering tax breaks and other incentives.

Wars between Central American nations have ended, and in place of armed conflict regional ties are being built. Business and government leaders in Costa Rica are talking to their counterparts in Panama. Guatemala is actively soliciting trade and investment from El Salvador and Costa Rica, as well as from South American nations. The border dispute between El Salvador and Honduras is at least tentatively settled.

Clearly Central America has begun the long trek out of the dark ages of isolationism. Civilian institutions are stronger than they have been for decades. Financial systems are beginning to function again. And intellectuals, politicians, and church leaders are beginning to establish dialogues and contacts at the international level. Although none of these improvements by itself will solve Central America's problems, together they are working to move the region closer to modern-day practices on a par with many of its Latin American neighbors.

Mexico differs markedly from both South America and Central America. Its relationship with the United States is strongly influenced by geographic proximity and the North American Free Trade Agreement (NAFTA). Culturally, this nation of mixed mestizo, Latin, and Amerindian ancestry tends to feel much closer to Guatemala, El Salvador, and other Central American nations than to South America.

Mexico has changed radically over the past twenty years. Maturation of its political process coupled with the enormous economic benefits of NAFTA has transformed this friendly neighbor of 100 million people from an inward-looking, isolated, oil-rich nation to a valuable partner of the United States in the global economy. Maquildoras are booming, and education reform is making inroads. Mexico is approaching the time when it will be considered a developed, not a developing, nation.

Government Regulation

Let's look at which countries are easiest to do business in from the perspective of government regulations. The International Finance Corporation, an arm of the World Bank, publishes an annual report, the latest edition of which is entitled *Doing Business in 2006: Creating Jobs*. This report measures the ease of doing business in 155 countries, given the government regulations in each country. It looks at ten criteria:

1. The ease of starting a business
2. Dealing with licenses
3. Hiring and firing workers
4. Registering property
5. Getting credit

6. Protecting investors
7. Paying taxes
8. Trading across borders
9. Enforcing contracts
10. Closing a business

This study shows that of all Latin American countries, Chile ranks at the top in ease of doing business. This means that overall, government regulations are less onerous there than anywhere else in the region. However, relative to the rest of the world, Chile ranks only twenty-fifth. In Latin America, Chile is followed by Jamaica, Panama, and surprisingly, Nicaragua. Nicaragua, however, ranked eightieth in the world in the ease of hiring and firing workers. Within this classification, the cost of hiring an employee was judged to be about 17 percent of wages paid and the cost of firing an employee a whopping twenty-four weeks of wages. For comparative purposes, note that the United States ranked third in the world in overall ease of doing business relative to government regulations and sixth in the ease of hiring and firing workers.

Table 4-1 | Ease of Doing Business 2006

	Rank Latin America	Rank World	Start a Business
United States	N/A	3	3
Chile	1	25	23
Jamaica	2	43	10
Panama	3	57	21
Nicaragua	4	59	65
Colombia	5	66	73
Peru	6	71	106
Mexico	7	73	84
El Salvador	8	76	127
Argentina	9	77	85
Paraguay	10	88	118
Uruguay	11	85	116
Costa Rica	12	89	83
Dominican Republic	13	103	101
Guyana	14	105	63
Ecuador	15	107	122
Guatemala	16	109	120
Bolivia	17	111	132
Honduras	18	112	129
Brazil	19	119	98
Venezuela	20	120	95

Deal with Licenses	Hiring/Firing	Register Property	Get Credit
17	6	12	15
35	37	30	32
82	39	95	92
62	115	55	19
72	80	110	71
46	130	50	62
97	83	32	73
49	125	74	68
75	88	45	34
103	132	65	42
104	137	52	54
38	52	126	60
43	72	38	33
33	100	116	47
61	N/A	25	145
45	129	102	81
142	92	61	49
52	89	109	79
79	56	78	50
115	144	105	80
96	71	47	76

Table 4-1—Continued | Ease of Doing Business 2006

	Protecting Investors	Paying Taxes
United States	7	30
Chile	36	63
Jamaica	59	141
Panama	92	93
Nicaragua	72	130
Colombia	37	148
Peru	21	133
Mexico	125	95
El Salvador	81	82
Argentina	51	143
Paraguay	43	71
Uruguay	76	144
Costa Rica	134	129
Dominican Republic	112	124
Guyana	101	65
Ecuador	113	86
Guatemala	122	125
Bolivia	98	146
Honduras	129	113
Brazil	53	140
Venezuela	142	145

Source: Doing Business in 2006: Creating Jobs, International Finance Corporation, World Bank

Trading Across Borders	Enforcing Contracts	Closing a Business
17	10	17
42	41	82
37	40	24
58	126	74
50	22	55
81	83	27
93	114	60
39	100	22
113	53	64
43	91	52
97	107	114
71	139	63
88	141	99
32	130	131
112	123	104
77	90	88
51	117	86
116	112	47
119	136	84
107	70	141
91	129	129

This report measures each country's regulatory burden. It is concerned with the time and cost associated with various government requirements and their effect on the business community. Government intervention in virtually all Latin American countries is one of the most onerous of the external market forces and the one that is the most difficult for companies to deal with. That makes this index a helpful tool in determining which market to go after. Equally important, it identifies which countries require extra effort to maneuver around government regulations. However, this ease-of-doing-business index does not take into consideration such economic and social conditions as macroeconomic policy, quality of infrastructure, currency volatility, investor perceptions, or crime rates. These factors may be more important than onerous government regulations.

Next, let's look at a selection of major-market countries.

Argentina

Argentina is a less complex business environment than Brazil but more difficult for American firms than Colombia, Chile, or Mexico. On the plus side, Argentine consumers are probably the most sophisticated in Latin America, and infrastructures are in pretty good shape.

Some of the hottest consumer exports to Argentina are sports oriented and include equipment, clothing, and accessories for soccer, water polo, horse racing, backpacking, yachting, and water sports. American-made computers, peripherals, software, and state-of-the-art electronic appliances are also in high demand. Drugs and health-care supplies sell very well there as they do throughout Latin America. Brand-name apparel, fast-food chains, physical fitness centers, compact discs, cellular phones, and all tourist-related products also do well. The best commercial/industrial markets are shown in **Table 4-2**.

Table 4-2 | Best Commercial/Industrial Markets for Export to Argentina

Product Line	Market Size 2004 ($ million)	Imports As Percent of Market
Telecommunications	1,400	97.6
Information technology	693	76.6
Agricultural machinery/parts	143	70.6
Medical equipment/supplies	236	66.1
Industrial chemicals	7,350	30.5

Source: U.S. Commercial Service

There are several negatives to doing business in Argentina. Thanks to Mercosur, imports from non-member countries like the United States carry a common external tariff of up to 22 percent, except for automobiles, which carry a tariff of 35 percent. The banking system is still recovering from the financial crisis created by a five-year financial recession, making in-country trade finance difficult to arrange. Travel and shipping distances from the United States are substantial. European traditions predominate and influence product design, advertising, and sales promotions. Local business cartels are hard to beat, and labor unions still have a high degree of control over both the workplace and the social fabric of the country.

Argentina has one of the strictest set of restrictions on imports in all of Latin America. Government regulations proliferate. You need government approval to import the following products into Argentina:

- Pharmaceuticals
- Foodstuffs
- Insecticides
- Veterinary products
- Medical devices
- Defense materials
- Cosmetics and toiletries
- Special vehicles

- Publications
- Shoes
- Carpets
- Paper

Such extensive government interference is the main reason Argentina ranks as low as it does in the ease-of-doing-business index. Here are Argentina's statistics summarized from tables previously presented:

Ease of doing business ranking within Latin America (out of 20 countries): 9

GDP per capita (PPP): $13,700

Population: 38.6 million

Literacy rate: 97%

Inflation rate: 12.3%

Global growth competitiveness ranking within Latin America (out of 21 countries): 11

Business competitiveness ranking within Latin America (out of 21 countries): 9

Corruption index within Latin America (10 is squeaky clean, 0 is awful): 2.8

Internet users: 10 million

Internet users percent of population: 25%

Gender gap ranking within Latin America (out of 9 countries): 4

Unemployment rate: 11.1%

Percent of population living in extreme poverty: 21%

Indigenous peoples percent of population: 3%

Health-care system ranking within Latin America (out of 20 countries): 12

The ranking of ninth in the business competitive index puts Argentina in the middle of Latin American countries. However, its inflation rate of 12.3 percent is much too high, making pricing especially difficult. The corruption index of 2.8 is much worse than in most other Latin American countries. In fact, only eight countries out of twenty-one are more corrupt than Argentina. The poverty rate is also unacceptable, with 21 percent of Argentines living in extreme poverty. This shows that the country is still recovering from the financial panic of November 2001. On the plus side, a gender gap ranking of four isn't too bad. Women do, in fact, have a reasonable say in both government and business. And with one out of four Argentines using the Internet, e-commerce might be a viable alternative sales strategy.

Market-entry in Argentina requires the use of sales representatives or distributors. Also, the entire business domain is based on personal relationships. You must take the time to be in Argentina and socialize with your representatives and distributors, not once a year, but many times during the year. Doing business in Argentina requires a very high level of participation by a U.S. exporter, including a lot of research, preparation, and personal involvement. Also, always use an in-country Argentine translator. Even though you may be fluent in Spanish, Argentine Spanish sounds a lot different than Mexican, Colombian, or Dominican Spanish.

Brazil

Brazil is certainly the most complex market in Latin America. It also has the largest consumer base with a wide range of consumer tastes. In fact, there are ten metropolitan areas whose populations each exceed 1 million people. It also boasts a diverse industrial base, and, as in most Latin markets, American goods are in demand. Since 2001, the cost of living has decreased, and 4.5 million jobs have been added to the economy. Eleven million families receive a minimum stipend in exchange for vaccinating their babies and keeping their children in school.

However, Brazil also has some big minuses. The local business base is firmly entrenched. Competition from U.S. and European companies, as well as from a thriving underground economy, is fierce. Markets in São Paulo, Rio de

Janeiro, Recife, Fortaleza, and the other metropolitan areas are quite different one from the other. Urban markets are very dissimilar from rural markets. The country's commercial laws are changing so rapidly that it's difficult to plan anything. And interest rates remain high.

Corruption in government seems to be increasing. Nearly 20 percent of congressional representatives in the lower house have been implicated in either a cash-for-votes scandal or a scheme to buy over-priced ambulances. Transparência Brasil reported in 2006 that 39 percent of the 496 members of this lower house face legal proceedings.

As a general rule, the government discourages imports of consumer goods, although virtually any made-in-the-USA product or a copy of it can be obtained in the underground economy. Consumer imports that are welcomed in the formal economy include virtually all health-care products, education supplies (including textbooks), electronic appliances, and American designer clothes. **Table 4-3** lists the best commercial/industrial product lines for export to Brazil.

Table 4-3 | Best Commercial/Industrial Markets for Export to Brazil

Product Line	Market Size 2004 ($ million)	Imports As Percent of Market
Safety/security equipment	1,150	50.4
Highway equipment/supplies	3,400	41.2
Computer hardware/software	37,000	40.5
Telecommunications equipment	6,300	38.9
Medical equipment	2,389	37.7
Pharmaceuticals	9,722	24.7
Electric power equipment	4,465	24.2
Construction equipment	563	26.5

Source: U.S. Commercial Service

Brazil has the twelfth largest economy and is the fifth most populous country in the world. It encompasses about half of South America's geography and economy. The United States is Brazil's second largest trading partner (after the European Union), with exports totaling about $14 billion in 2005. Rich in a variety of agriculture products and natural resources, Brazil also has a world-renowned industrial base. Automobiles, steel, petrochemicals, and computers are major industries.

Trade shows provide one of the best ways to enter a new market in Brazil. Many, many trade shows are offered throughout the year in all major cities. You will need a Brazilian partner, however. Joint ventures are very popular, although you can get by with a Brazilian sales representative or distributor. Brazil's business culture is based on personal relationships. That means if you don't have an in-country presence, at least a sales office, you will not be in a position to communicate personally with bureaucrats, customers, and suppliers. By all means open a sales office and, if possible, form a joint venture with your representative or distributor. This will ensure that Brazilians regard you as a permanent fixture in the business community and not merely another American company testing the waters.

Although no one can dispute that Brazil offers the largest and most varied markets in Latin America, there are also some negatives. Rural Brazilians continue to migrate to the cities creating, among other ills, a large base of unemployed, unskilled workers. Brazil has one of the most unequal distributions of wealth in the world. This results in significant crime, drug abuse, health epidemics, and poor public education. Brazil also suffers from significant environmental degradation, especially in its rain forest. Here are summarized statistics from tables previously presented.

Ease of doing business ranking within Latin America (out of 20 countries): 19

GDP per capita (PPP): $8,400

Population: 186 million

Literacy rate: 86%

Inflation rate: 5.7%

Global growth competitiveness ranking within Latin America (out of 21 countries): 8

Business competitiveness ranking within Latin America (out of 21 countries): 2

Corruption index within Latin America: 3.7

Internet users: 25.9 million

Internet users percent of population: 14%

Gender gap ranking within Latin America (out of 9 countries): 8

Unemployment rate: 9.9%

Percent of population living in extreme poverty: 13%

Indigenous peoples percent of population: 0.5%

Health-care system ranking within Latin America (out of 20 countries): 17

Brazil is ranked nineteenth in the ease-of-doing-business category. That's nineteenth out of twenty countries. Only Venezuela has more onerous government regulations to deal with. But the business competitiveness ranking, which includes non-regulatory factors, places Brazil in the number-two slot. The corruption index of 3.7 puts Brazil about in the middle of all Latin countries. The gender gap rank of eighth out of nine countries does not speak well for the treatment of women in this society. Very few women have the opportunity to engage in meaningful political or economic activities, something to definitely recognize in your strategic marketing plans.

Thirteen percent of Brazilians live in extreme poverty. For a country whose population tops 186 million people, 24.5 million people living in extreme poverty boggles the mind. Since indigenous peoples are a mere one-half of 1 percent of the population, such a large number of very poor people reflects the sad state of the unemployed and underemployed in the ten largest cities. Moreover, a country whose health-care system is ranked seventeenth out of twenty countries clearly needs a massive overhaul of its medical and pharmaceutical industries. Still, Brazil's size makes it a tempting morsel. Such large markets influence U.S. companies to continue exporting to the country and investing in its commercial/industrial base, despite the many obstacles they encounter.

Chile

Chile, which ranks first in the ease-of-doing-business index, has become the darling of many U.S. companies, mainly because it offers far and away the most open markets to imports and is the furthest along in its economic reforms. Consumer tastes run pro-American. Shopping malls are very popular. And credit-card use is increasing daily. Chile is arguably the most trade-and-investment-friendly country in Latin America. Its markets are growing. Its citizens are relatively well educated, at least those living in the cities. Its political climate remains as stable as any in the region.

Chile's growth rate hovers between 5 percent and 6 percent, significantly higher than the average 2 to 3 percent growth rate in the United States. The U.S.-Chile Free Trade Agreement was put in place January 1, 2004, permitting about 90 percent of U.S. goods to enter Chile unencumbered by any tariffs. Tariffs for the remaining 10 percent will be phased out by 2015. Chile has also forged free-trade agreements with Canada, Mexico, the Central American nations, the European Union, and South Korea and, as of this writing, is negotiating agreements with China, India, New Zealand, and Singapore.

The biggest problem faced by new U.S. exporters to Chilean markets is competition, not only from in-country businesses, but also from European, Asian, and U.S. companies. Hundreds of American companies have already taken advantage of Chile's open markets and the U.S.-Chile Free Trade Agreement and are vigorously pursuing increased shares of a variety of markets. Total U.S. exports to Chile in 2004 increased about 35 percent over the previous year.

I believe that everyone who has done business in this country would agree that the key to success is finding a Chilean partner with the right connections. A Chilean sales representative or distributor can open government doors and make business and social connections, so necessary for moving your products smoothly and efficiently to market. Moreover, any foreign corporation may open a Chilean office under its own name. This is a rarity in Latin America, and you should not overlook it in your strategic marketing plans.

Unfortunately, as in every Latin American country, the piracy of intellectual property remains a serious hurdle. If this is of critical concern to your company, perhaps you should stay away from Chile and even Latin America in general. Here are Chile's statistics summarized from tables previously presented.

Ease of doing business ranking within Latin America (out of 20 countries): 1

GDP per capita (PPP): $11,300

Population: 15.1 million

Literacy rate: 96%

Inflation rate: 3.2%

Global growth competitiveness ranking within Latin America (out of 21 countries): 1

Business competitiveness ranking within Latin America (out of 21 countries): 1

Corruption index within Latin America: 7.3

Internet users: 5.6 million

Internet users percent of population: 35%

Gender gap ranking within Latin America (out of 9 countries): 6

Unemployment rate: 8%

Percent of population living in extreme poverty: 5%

Indigenous peoples percent of population: 3%

Health-care system ranking within Latin America (out of 20 countries): 2

Chile is not only ranked number 1 in the ease-of-doing-business index, it is also ranked number 1 for global growth competitiveness and business competitiveness and number 2 for its health-care system. It didn't do as well in the empowerment of women, however, ranking only sixth out of nine. This seems strange considering that a woman has been elected president of the country.

The fact that 5 percent of the population lives in extreme poverty indicates that the government has its work cut out to increase jobs and income for this impoverished class Also, be aware that in addition to intense competition, marine shipping routes from the United States are very long, and Chile's geography makes reaching markets other than Santiago very difficult. This long, thin country is 4,000 miles long and 100 miles wide.

Chileans are fast becoming modern consumers, demanding a wide range of imports, especially those made in America. The list includes, but is certainly not limited to cosmetics, women's work and dress clothes, leather goods, dried and frozen foods, low-priced toys, furniture of all types, health-care and personal-care products, electronic and electric appliances, personal security and safety devices, costume jewelry, sporting equipment and accessories, and many more items. According to the U.S. Commerical Service, the best commercial/industrial products for export to Chile are shown in **Table 4-4**.

Table 4-4 | Best Markets for Exports to Chile

Product Line	Market Size ($ million)	Imports As Percent of Market
Computer hardware/software	521	52.8
Food processing/packaging equipment	183	51.4
Medical equipment	78	32.1
Construction equipment	563	26.5
Mining equipment	338	21.9

Source: U.S. Commercial Service

Colombia

Colombia tends to be overlooked by U.S. companies because of the extensive publicity given to gangland-type killings, nefarious drug trafficking, and kidnappings. However, only occasionally do such activities touch foreigners. With recent changes in trade and foreign direct investment laws and a new free-trade agreement with the United States, Colombia's potential for U.S. companies looks promising. Upper- and middle-class markets are expanding rapidly. U.S. dollars are in plentiful supply to pay for American imports. Shipping distances from the United States are not much greater than to Trinidad and Tobago or Panama, and Colombia continues to be the most fiscally sound country in the region.

But there are risks. Cartels, or *sindicatos*, flourish. (*Sindicatos* are firms linked through a tight web of cross-holdings, in the same vein as the Japanese *keiretsu*.) Thirty-five percent of Colombia's population lives in rural areas with incomes too low to purchase imported goods. Travel and shipping lanes among the six urban centers can be difficult to navigate. And, although the government encourages foreign trade, Colombian consumers are not yet totally sold on American-made goods in preference to locally produced products.

Colombia is the third most populous country in Latin America, after Brazil and Mexico. Thirty cities have populations of 100,000 or more. Unlike the rest of Latin America, Colombia has not suffered any dramatic economic collapses or fiscal panics. It boasts a stable government and close business ties to the United States.

Although Colombia's population of 46 million is greater than that of Argentina's, consumer markets have not traditionally been favorite targets of U.S. exporters. But regional pressures to open the economy are causing this to change. The best prospects for consumer exports include automotive parts and accessories; health care and personal care products; processed foods; computers, peripherals, and software; cellular phones; travel and tourism products and services; and dress apparel. The best prospects for commercial/industrial products and services according to the U.S. Commercial Service are shown in **Table 4-5**.

Table 4-5 | Best Commercial/Industrial Markets for Exports to Colombia

Product Line	Market Size ($ million)	Imports as Percent of Market
Information Technology	975	99.5
Oil/Gas Machinery and Services	1,360	95.6
Plastic Materials/Supplies	1,48	70.8
Construction/Mining Equipment/Supplies	310	98.4
Electric Power Systems	418	88.8
Processed Food	3,350	23.6

Source: U.S. Commercial Service

Although slighted in the past, Colombia has now become the fourth largest Latin American trading partner for the United States, after Mexico, Brazil, and Venezuela. Several major projects that will require foreign direct investment and foreign goods and services are in the works. Here is a very abbreviated list: road, port, and airport construction; oil and gas exploration; railways; water treatment and supply facilities; electric power generation; mass transit systems; and security and defense products and services. Bear in mind, however, that the government is the main customer for these markets. To sell to the government, you must have a local presence or an agent who can legally bind your company to contracts. This is a very dangerous strategy. Unless you also have your own supervisor on premises, a local agent could enact legally binding contracts that would seriously damage your company.

While on that subject, be aware that formality, personal relationships, and trust are crucial when negotiating contracts. Colombians demand efficient after-sale customer service. If you don't warrant your products, do not come to Colombia. Here are Colombia's statistics summarized from tables previously presented.

Ease of doing business ranking within Latin America (out of 20 countries): 5

GDP per capita (PPP): $7,100

Population: 46 million

Literacy rate: 93%

Inflation rate: 4.9%

Global growth competitiveness ranking within Latin America (out of 21 countries): 5

Business competitiveness ranking within Latin America (out of 21 countries): 5

Corruption index within Latin America: 4

Internet users: 3.6 million

Internet users percent of population: 8%

Gender gap ranking within Latin America (out of 9 countries): 2

Unemployment rate: 10.2%

Percent of population living in extreme poverty: 24%

Indigenous peoples percent of population: 4%

Health-care system ranking within Latin America (out of 20 countries): 1

Colombia's ranking of fifth on the ease-of-doing-business scale speaks well for the changes that have occurred in the business community during the last ten years. When gangs of thugs roamed the roads and city streets and drug lords ruled the day, doing business in Colombia was anything but easy. Now that has changed. The business community is flourishing and the government did what had to be done to get the gangs under control. Colombia's global growth competitiveness rank of fifth verifies how much has changed. Women do very well in Colombia, both in the political sphere and in business. Also, the Colombian health-care system is the best in the region. That's a lot of positives for a country all but written off by American business in the 1990s.

Costa Rica

Costa Rica is significantly different from the rest of Central America. While the other countries were embroiled in civil wars (except for Panama and Belize), put up with military repression and political violence from their own governments, and suffered severe economic hardships, Costa Ricans have enjoyed relative peace and prosperity. Today, while its neighbors struggle for political and economic stability, Costa Rica stands like a beacon in the night as a shining example of how a tiny country can, with determination, withstand the winds of turmoil and become a model to be emulated by the rest of the Caribbean Basin.

In 1948, Costa Rica abolished its army in favor of a Civil Guard. During modern times, the nation's only flirtation with war came in 1955, when a rebel force based in Nicaragua attempted an invasion to overthrow the government.

With assistance from the Organization of America States, the government quickly put down the rebels.

With free elections, the absence of any military organization, high levels of literacy, and extensive social welfare programs, 3.3 million Costa Ricans have lived a peaceful but nervous existence since the early 1980s. During that violent decade, the government became overburdened with external debt and a bloated bureaucracy. This caused severe economic strains, and many Costa Ricans saw their standard of living decline. Also, Costa Rica could not completely insulate itself from nearby civil uprisings. Refugees from war-torn neighbor states regularly flooded in. And, as if to demonstrate that no country is immune from the drug scourge, international narcotics traffickers have increasingly used Costa Rican territory as a stopover between South America and the United States (although this isn't as severe a problem as it is in Guatemala).

A growing antagonism toward refugees has soured many Costa Ricans on forming closer economic, political, or financial ties with other Central American nations. For this reason, DR-CAFTA has always been of questionable value for Costa Rica.

The second smallest Central American nation (its area is about the size of Vermont and New Hampshire combined), Costa Rica lies between Nicaragua on the north and Panama on the south. As is the case in other Central American countries, the Costa Rican landscape comprises tropical coastal lowlands facing the Pacific Ocean and the Caribbean Sea, a ridge of the Antillean mountain range, and a large central plateau. One of its volcanoes, Mount Irazú, rises more than 11,000 feet, and from its peak one can see both the Pacific and the Caribbean coasts. About 75 percent of the country is forested, and a large part has been set aside by the government as national park land.

As is the case in all of Latin America, data from government sources tends to be sketchy and somewhat out of date.

However, here are Costa Rica's statistics summarized from tables previously presented.

Ease of doing business ranking within Latin America (out of 20 countries): 12

GDP per capita (PPP): $10,100

Population: 4 million

Literacy rate: 96%

Inflation rate: 13.8%

Global growth competitiveness ranking within Latin America (out of 21 countries): 7

Business competitiveness ranking within Latin America (out of 21 countries): 3

Corruption index within Latin America: 4.2

Internet users: 1 million

Internet users percent of population: 24%

Gender gap ranking within Latin America (out of 9 countries): 1

Unemployment rate: 6.6%

Percent of population living in extreme poverty: 8%

Indigenous peoples percent of population: 1%

Health-care system ranking within Latin America (out of 21 countries): 3

Although Costa Rica is twelfth on the ease-of-doing-business scale, it has many other positive features. The global growth competitiveness ranking of 7 is excellent as is its business competitiveness ranking of three. A corruption index of 4.2 is the third best in the region, behind only Chile (7.3) and Uruguay (5.9.) Twenty-four percent of the population uses the Internet, making e-commerce a viable alternative sales tool. Costa Rica ranks at the top of the list in the gender gap index, meaning that Costa Rican women have more empowerment than women in any other Latin American country, both in the government and in business. Only 8 percent of the population lives in extreme poverty. This is a very low percentage compared to other Latin countries. And third place in the health-care system ranking promises a ready market for medical and hospital equipment and supplies.

Costa Rica has a very small industrial base, so nearly all commercial and industrial products must be imported. The best lines for export from the United States are paper and paperboard products ($272 million market size), agricultural chemicals ($178 million market), automobile parts and accessories ($166 million market), plastic materials and resins ($155 million market), information technology equipment and software ($131 million market), and telecommunications equipment and supplies ($130 million market).

Mexico

NAFTA gave Mexico a new lease on life. Imports from the United States skyrocketed in 2005 to a whopping $120 billion. In fact, the United States now accounts for 75 percent of all Mexican trade, and Mexico is the second largest trading partner of the United States, after Canada. Many reforms that make the Mexican government more transparent and accountable have been pushed through in the past five years.

The maquiladora industry (maquiladoras are otherwise known as *twin plants*) has thousands of assembly plants near the U.S. border producing products for export back to the United States. A large number of U.S. companies find these maquiladoras an excellent way to produce goods at a lower labor cost without incurring long-distance shipping costs. And with NAFTA-reduced tariffs, the movement of goods back and forth across the border is easily and economically accomplished.

It's difficult to come up with a list of best products for export to Mexico. Indeed, the diverse markets in this large country demand everything that Americans buy in their supermarkets and shopping malls. Be aware, however, that

Mexicans are very price conscious and appreciate good service. Take your time learning the ways of this vast country, and before long you'll be doing business like a native.

The education system is one segment of the economy that cries out for U.S. goods and services. Mexico is the most populous Spanish-speaking country in the world and the second most populous country in Latin America, second only to Brazil. About 70 percent of its non-indigenous citizens live in urban areas. One result of this demographic is that the Mexican government has given education its highest priority, significantly increasing the education budget for several years running. In fact, education expenditures increased more than 25 percent over the past decade.

Mexico is now decentralizing education, shifting responsibility from the federal government to the states to improve accountability. Schooling is mandatory from ages six through eighteen, plus one year of pre-kindergarten. By the millennium, 94 percent of children age six to fourteen were enrolled in school. Such emphasis on education makes Mexico unique in Latin America. It also offers an enormous market for equipment and supplies needed to run the schools.

The majority of Mexican private schools now teach English as part of the required curriculum. English as a second language (ESL) has also been introduced in some public high schools. Gradually, the government plans to install these programs in all high, middle, and elementary public schools. This offers an excellent opportunity for American teachers with ESL training.

So much for education. Here are Mexico's statistics summarized from tables previously presented.

Ease of doing business ranking within Latin America (out of 20 countries): 7

GDP per capita (PPP): $10,100

Population: 105 million

Literacy rate: 89%

Inflation rate: 3.3%

Global growth competitiveness ranking within Latin America (out of 21 countries): 3

Business competitiveness ranking within Latin America (out of 21 countries): 7

Corruption index within Latin America: 3.5

Internet users: 17 million

Internet users percent of population: 16%

Gender gap ranking within Latin America (out of 9 countries): 9

Unemployment rate: 3.6%

Percent of population living in extreme poverty: 13%

Indigenous peoples percent of population: 30%

Health-care system ranking within Latin America (out of 20 countries): 8

As the two indexes, ease-of-doing-business and business competitiveness indicate, doing business in Mexico is fairly easy compared with the other Latin American countries. If you take your time, establish personal relationships, and pay attention to competition, you should do all right. Although corruption has not vanished, it is not as pronounced in Mexico as it is in other Latin American countries. Also, the high number of Internet users might make e-commerce a viable alternative for in-country marketing.

On the downside, about 13 percent of Mexicans live in extreme poverty, an unacceptable condition. Clearly, the government hasn't paid enough attention to this large segment of the population, especially to the 30 million indigenous peoples. One of the most surprising weaknesses on Mexican landscape is the country's gender gap ranking. Out of nine countries in the survey, Mexico ranks dead last in empowering women. This is a serious shortcoming. Women represent half the population or about 52 million citizens. After reducing this number by about 15 million indigenous women, almost 40 million non-indigenous women are not afforded anything close to equal opportunities with men. If you deal in consumer products, your strategic marketing plans must take this wide gap into consideration when defining Mexican markets.

Conclusion

Latin America's turbulent past has created a surfeit of market risks that any foreign company wishing to do business in this region must recognize and deal with. Market risks in a specific country or a particular region or city within that country are not always transparent. While some conditions are glaringly obvious, others are more subtle.

When you develop your Latin American marketing strategies, keep in mind four points:

1. Dig deep enough to uncover the unique characteristics of each country, and then match these characteristics to regional cultural traits and demographic trends
2. Although middle-class consumers may not be as sophisticated and demanding as those from upper classes, they still want high-quality goods at reasonable prices.
3. Host-country producers, underground-market dealers, and European and Asian companies provide stiff competition.
4. A wide range of political, social, and economic forces that are not encountered in U.S. markets, may, in the end, separate those marketing policies that will work from those that will not work.

Chapter 5

Latin Traits That Baffle Americans

A few years ago, I was the keynote speaker at the annual conference of a large trade association. Many people in the audience had been doing business in Latin America for more than twenty years. After dinner, one member who was about my age and had started his Latin American career in Venezuela, had worked in most Latin countries, and was now heading a start-up venture in Guatemala, asked, "What do you mean by cultural risks? I know about culture clash, cultural differences, and cultural traits, but I've never heard of cultural risks." My rather long-winded explanation went something like this.

"Anyone doing business in a foreign land must adjust his or her behavior to local customs and mores. We all know that. However, more and more it seems that Americans abroad tend to believe that everyone, all over the world, should accept their behavior as typically American and not take offense if what they say or do differs from local customs. With all the publicity international trade has had in the last fifteen years, this surprises me. Yet, my experience has been that once American businesspeople, male or female, step on foreign soil, they forget about any cross-cultural training they may have had and jump right into a business situation with the same vigor and lack of courtesy that they exhibit at home. This seems to be especially true of the younger generation and of businesswomen more than businessmen.

"Why do conflicts arise? Because either we do not understand the customs and mores of our hosts or we do not respect those differences. After all, and this we must always remember, we are guests in that country. As guests, we should honor the cultural diversity of our host as we would honor the desires of our host at a dinner party back home.

"At any rate, when Americans start out in a new overseas market, and especially in Latin America, they face enormous external market risks. But they also face significant differences in customs and mores that create conflicts and jeopardize success as much as corruption, street crime, or government interference. That's what I mean by cultural risks."

The Latin American cultural traits that seem to give U.S. businesspeople the greatest difficulty evolve either from the region's Hispanic heritage or from its past experiences. Much of what I discuss in this chapter relates to Latin America as a whole but not necessarily those Caribbean countries with a strong West Indian culture. Also, some characteristics are more pronounced in one country or sub-region than another, and I will try to highlight those as we come to them.

One of the hardest lessons for newcomers to Latin America to learn is that generalizations about anything, but especially about people, are always wrong. Nowhere is this truer than in the nebulous area of local customs. The beliefs of a friend from England who lived in northern New Jersey for eight years are a good example. During that time, all she had seen of the United States was north Jersey and Manhattan. When her sister from England visited her one Christmas, I overheard my friend make the following comments about our American culture.

"Americans are rude, uncaring, and self-centered. They are always in a hurry to get somewhere. And boy, are they violent. You can't walk down the street without being accosted by a bum or a teenage junkie. Date rape is endemic here, so when you go out, regardless of how well you know the man, be sure to carry mace in your purse; all American women do. And never carry your purse on your shoulder or you'll likely be mugged, even in broad daylight."

This was the same woman who wouldn't believe me when I explained that most Americans pumped their own gas. (New Jersey was one of two states with laws against self-service gas stations.) She had never ventured outside her New York/New Jersey cocoon, had never visited Eugene, Oregon, or Biloxi, Mississippi, or Duluth, Minnesota. Yet she firmly believed that she understood the American culture inside out. After all, hadn't she lived here for eight years?

A similar experience occurred during the time that I owned a manufacturing company in the Midwest. We had a new Guatemalan customer, and I decided to pay him a visit. I took my marketing manager on his first international sales call to introduce him to Latin business. From Guatemala City, we took a bus to Puerto Barrios on the Caribbean coast, then a boat to Livingston.

Boarding the plane for home, I asked his opinion of the six-day trip. He answered:

"I hope I never have to make another trip to Latin America." He didn't even restrict his judgment to Guatemala or Central America. "The people are all snobs or drunks. I didn't trust anyone we negotiated with. We should have wrapped up this trip in three days, not six, but the pace is so slow you can't get anything done. And I don't understand why we had to have an interpreter. Didn't these people understand we are Americans and that they should speak English?"

Talk about an ugly American. This man didn't have to worry about returning to Guatemala. I would never let him ruin our business there with that kind of attitude. As it turned out, two weeks later I fired him.

Many cultural characteristics endemic to Latin America are shaped by political events, economic standing, religious beliefs, racial mixture, education levels, and a variety of other factors. These vary region by region and country by country within a region. For lack of a better term, I call these attributes experiential traits.

Other cultural traits stem more from a Hispanic heritage. These I call heritage traits. They appear over and over again, regardless of the specific country. Although the degree of visibility of these traits varies considerably from one place to the next, they seem immune to change from religious pressures, economic status, or the influence of indigenous peoples or other cultures.

The most important heritage traits to incorporate in your strategic marketing plans include the following:

- A high regard for family values
- An easy-going, live-and-let-live attitude
- A respect for age
- Excessive community involvement
- Sharp class separation

Let's begin by examining the role of the family in every-day Latin life and see how it affects attitudes toward business, politics, and social activities.

Family Values

Latin Americans from a Hispanic or mestizo background place a strong emphasis on family values. Daily life centers on the family, not the individual. Some people define the family group as immediate relatives, that is, mother, father, and children. But many families extend well beyond this close-knit group. These extended families include distant relatives, like grandparents, cousins, nieces and nephews and, of course, everyone's spouses.

The term *family* can also refer to neighborhoods and entire communities. Athletic teams, churches, and small businesses may include members from several families living in close proximity. The bonds that hold this type of extended family together are as strong as those that bind mother, father, and children.

Nearly all activities, including shopping, focus on one aspect or another of family life. For example, Latin Americans purchase television sets under the assumption that family and friends will gather to watch their favorite programs. Cars are purchased knowing that all family members will drive or ride in them. Lower-income families purchase clothing, shoes, and accessories under the assumption that they will be handed down from one family member to another.

When developing your marketing plan for consumer goods, it's important to incorporate this bent toward family sharing. Emphasize the value of your product to the family, not the individual. Such emphasis is particularly important when selling products for the younger generation, such as clothing, athletic equipment, toys, snack food, and so on.

Speaking of the younger generation, the Latin culture teaches that children need adult protection and guidance. They are expected to accept the judgment of their parents about what is good for them and what is not. Contrary to the American culture, children are not considered little adults, able to make up their own minds as consumers. Remember, products that appeal to young people in the United States may not necessarily appeal to parents of young people in Latin America, with certain exceptions, of course, such as jeans, sneakers, and hamburgers. When developing your sales promotions, be sure to emphasize your product's intrinsic value to young people, not just its pleasure-fulfilling worth.

Easy-Going Lifestyle

Life is a lot slower in Latin America than it is in the States. Yes, Mexico City, Guatemala City, São Paulo, and Santiago streets are jammed with traffic. This seems to be the case in metropolitan areas the world over. However, fewer media distractions, slower and more difficult transportation, and warmer climates tend to slow the pace of everyday life. This more relaxed lifestyle, plus the natural Latin affinity for leisure pursuits, leads to a laid-back attitude about virtually everything.

This can be a frustrating experience for the first-time business traveler to the region. We Americans have a tendency to want to move quickly, get the job done, close the order, and be on our way to the next meeting. Anything that slows us down becomes an irritant to be squelched as rapidly as possible. After all, we have deadlines to meet, commitments to fulfill, planes to catch. We set a time for a meeting or appointment and expect other parties to be there at that time. Moreover, if the meeting is supposed to end at noon, we expect it to end at noon so we can make our luncheon appointment. We don't have time to exchange pleasantries and chitchat. If you take that tack in Latin America, I guarantee you will not get the job done or close the order. Don't book a return flight. You'll never make it.

In any Latin American country, business dealings are based on personal, one-on-one relationships. Latinos want to get to know you. They want to know how your family is, the acceptability of your hotel accommodations, and most important, your reaction to their lovely country. Conversely, Latin Americans expect you to have the same interest in them. They expect you to ask about their family, their health, and their interpretation of events occurring in their country. This last point warrants further explanation. As we'll see a little later, Latin Americans are very proud people. That pride begins with a strong nationalistic bias, regardless of the difficulties their countries may have encountered in the past or are experiencing now.

Dealing with this laid-back attitude absorbs an inordinate amount of time. But if you are not willing to ignore the clock like the rest of Latin Americans, you shouldn't do business anywhere in the region. To succeed, you must be ready and willing to move slowly, to go with the flow rather than to push forward to quick conclusions. This holds true whether negotiating a contract, selling a product, handling customer complaints, or dealing with government officials.

A Live-and-Let-Live Attitude

A corollary to this easy-going attitude is the way Latin Americans feel about outsiders encroaching on what they consider to be private matters. They don't like it. It may seem strange that people who are accustomed to what we would consider unconscionable interference in their everyday lives by hordes of bureaucrats and military desperados feel so strongly about personal liberties. Yet, Latin Americans have inherited a free-spirit outlook on life reminiscent of the flamboyant lifestyles of old-style Spanish courts and landed gentry.

On one hand, they acquiesce to overbearing authority figures. On the other hand, they prefer to live their personal lives as if there were no tomorrow. A good reflection of this live-for-today-and-tomorrow-be-damned attitude can be found in the dismal savings rates throughout the region. One reason for this is that people spend today because tomorrow their money may lose its value to inflation, as many have so often experienced in the past. This is certainly a relevant factor. However, from my experience, the free-spirit mentality that permeates the region is an even stronger motivation to spend rather than save. Planning is not one of their strong suits.

It's also important to keep in mind that many issues of the day that make Americans paranoid, such as smoking, abortion, drug use, sex, AIDS, personal safety, and so on, are non-issues in Latin America. This is not to say that as a group, Latin Americans are either for or against these issues. Nor is it to say that for certain people, one or more of these public issues are not critically important. But in Latin America, people are not paranoid about them. These issues are considered to be personal matters. Latinos don't want an outsider—outside the family, that is—telling them what they can do and what they can't do with their lives. They don't get hung up on social issues like we do. They take things as they come and roll with the punches.

I have encountered many Latinos who laugh (usually behind our backs) at the lengths to which our federal and state governments go in the name of personal safety. Take, for example, our preoccupation with seat belts and air bags. Anyone who has traveled much in Central America has at one time or another seen or even ridden in so-called *chicken buses*. For thousands of peasants and others living in rural areas, these buses are the only means of transportation. They roam the countryside stopping to pick up people or them drop off at will. Bus riders carry broken-down luggage, huge boxes, open food parcels, animals, and chickens—hence the name *chicken bus*. Of course these buses do not have air conditioning. Watching a chicken bus roll by you'll see children, chickens, mothers, goats, fathers, grandparents, and virtually every other living thing known to man hanging from windows and in some cases riding on top of the bus. Can you imagine the chaos and ridicule that would follow a government pronouncement that everyone not wearing a seat belt will be fined?

Or take smoking. Americans have grown so paranoid about secondhand smoke that many municipal laws now forbid smoking in any public area, including bars. New York City even tried to ban smoking in Central Park. Members of the U.S. military cannot smoke in any base enclosure. Can you imagine what would happen if, for example, Guatemala were to forbid indigenous Mayas in the outlying provinces from smoking in the few buildings left standing? Or sailor's bars in Puerto Barrios or Livingston put up no-smoking signs? If Latin Americans ever needed a reason to start a revolution, a ban on smoking would certainly do the trick.

Choosing to use drugs is also considered a personal matter. Marijuana plants, coca plants, and poppies can be found in abundance in many Latin American rural areas. Surreptitious processing facilities perk merrily along in remote mountain villages. Although pushing drugs is against the law, the use of marijuana, especially, is quite common. Picture, if you will, what might happen if the police, many of whom also use drugs, were directed to arrest and imprison anyone smoking marijuana. Jails couldn't be built fast enough to hold even a small percentage of detainees. And most judges would throw the cases out of court as frivolous.

Non-marital sex is also considered a personal matter, not to be constrained by superfluous laws. Although most married men and women that I know are monogamous, even they, on occasion, take sexual flings. Singles, and particularly single men, still harbor the belief that macho means sexual prowess and are out to prove it every chance they get. Of course, large families continue to be the norm, so if children result from these flings, no one objects too much. Hardly anyone uses contraceptives. In fact, they are not available in most villages and farming areas. As we saw in Chapter 3, HIV/AIDS continues to be a problem throughout Latin America, as it is in the rest of the world. But this doesn't seem to stop a casual indulgence now and then.

Most Latin Americans are romantic. Many smoke. And some occasionally use drugs. But they do not worry about what other people do. They have a live-and-let-live attitude. When you go there, I advise you to do as the locals do and leave your American hang-ups at home.

Respect for Age

Respect for the elderly is another common cultural trait that can be attributed to both Hispanic and mestizo heritages. In direct contrast to the American culture, Latin Americans regard elderly people as wise, experienced, and worth listening to. This trait undoubtedly is an offshoot of their high regard for families. Most family groups are ruled by the eldest male member; that is, they are patriarchal. This doesn't mean that the eldest female member doesn't have any say in family decisions. On the contrary, males may be the titular heads, but women normally rule the roost and must be consulted about decisions affecting the everyday lives of family members.

A reverence for the elderly will impact your marketing strategies in two ways. First, if at all possible, send senior marketing personnel rather than juniors to negotiate orders or contracts, whether you're buying or selling. The same holds true for setting up an offshore facility. Instruct one of your older managers to make the initial contacts with bureaucrats, potential sales representatives, and labor agents.

Even if your venture into this region is a minor part of your overall business plan, you will save money, time, and confusion by letting senior people go there first. This can be a particularly beneficial ploy when the people on the other side of the table are middle-aged or young. Your balding, gray-bearded senior will always have the initial edge in any business deal.

Second, if you have to send your own people to train local managers or workers, the older they are the better. Age commands respect. Age implies wisdom. Young Turks from the local community will listen more intently to and follow instructions more readily from an elder statesman. On the other hand, if you must send younger people on temporary assignment, then by all means send an older person along as an assistant, or, from the Latin vantage point, a chaperone.

This respect for age is a foreign concept in the United States. Here, age does not connote wisdom. Yes, the elderly are granted senior discounts to many events and yes, pharmaceutical companies create many special drugs for seniors. By and large, however, America's youth-oriented society tends to ignore the elderly. They are not granted the reverence that they are in Latin cultures.

However, it's not important how Americans view the elderly but how Latin Americans regard them. Americans who come to Latin America and treat the elderly as they are treated in the United States will fail in practically any business transaction.

The moral to all this? When in Rome, do as the Romans do. In Latin America, when dealing with a customer, supplier, or government official who is clearly your elder, put on your kid gloves, restrain your impatience, and respect that person's age.

Age also refers to companies. Relatively new companies that do not have longevity in their home markets will have a harder time marketing anywhere in Latin America than will companies that have been around a long time. No one wants to do business with the new kid on the block. After 1989, in what were the early days of expanded regional trade, too many unknown American companies jumped into the fray. What was perceived as terrific growth markets turned out to be markets too difficult to enter, with margins too meager and external market forces too strong to make the venture pay off. A quick evacuation by the Americans soured many Latin businesspeople and bureaucrats and contributed to the growing public opinion that the United States regarded the countries of Latin America as third-rate business partners.

Community Involvement

Community involvement is a mainstay of Latin life. Not infrequently, that involvement centers on the local church. Years of political violence, civil wars, and economic depredation have forced people even closer to their community church than they were two or three decades ago. A little later we'll take a look at the strong role religion plays in everyday life. For now, however, suffice to say that as a cohesive force that draws people together into a practicing community, the church stands tall.

Most Americans are probably not familiar with the term *community* as used in this context. We live in apartment or condo complexes, suburban developments, or neighborhoods of single-family homes. Often we live there for years without knowing our neighbors, beyond saying hello now and then. We explain this by saying we value our privacy. We would help if anyone needed it, but otherwise, let us enjoy our quiet comfort.

Don't get me wrong. We are not immune to the needs of our neighbors. In emergencies, we have a tradition of banding together for the good of the community. Witness the Midwest's Red River floods or Hurricane Andrew in Florida or the Los Angeles earthquake or Hurricane Katrina in Louisiana and Mississippi, when neighbors helped neighbors save their meager belongings and recover from horrendous catastrophes. Or look what happened in April 1995, when a renegade militiaman bombed the federal building in Oklahoma City, killing nearly 200 people. Assistance from as far away as Alaska, Hawaii, Florida, and Maine poured in to help uncover bodies and comfort survivors. Or even more recently, on September 11, 2001, when the World Trade Center towers in New York were destroyed and the Pentagon was severely damaged. Thousands of Americans rushed to help wherever they could.

Without an emergency, however, we are not usually this community minded.

The same cannot be said of Latin Americans. They don't need earthquakes, hurricanes, or bombings to bring neighbors together. They already are together, sharing, communicating with, and supporting one another. *Community* in the Latin sense means a common goal, namely, the survival or betterment of the group as a whole, without regard to individual desires. If the group survives or improves its economic standing, so does each individual family in the community. It is this togetherness that has stymied attempts to subdue the villages of indigenous peoples. When soldiers destroy one village, another one rises from the ashes. When mountain guerilla fighters are killed off, others from nearby villages take their places.

Latin Americans in general have a strong sense of community in everything they do. There is an important lesson in this for companies with strategic plans to open in-country manufacturing plants, distribution centers, or other facilities, even sales offices. The more you can do to convince customers, suppliers, employees, and bureaucrats that you have the same strong sense of community they have, the fewer obstacles will block your road. This may mean regular visits to municipal officials. It may mean sponsoring a community sports team. It may mean attending state functions, funerals, weddings, or church picnics. Whatever it takes, do it. You can't go wrong, and you'll likely find that getting involved in the community pushes aside the maze of regulations that every country imposes.

Class Separation

All Latin Americans are class conscious. In the more developed areas such as Buenos Aires or São Paulo, class lines are drawn according to job position, company or government affiliation, income, and the normal status symbols one finds in developed nations. However, in underdeveloped regions, race and gender seem to be the main determinants of class standing.

Racial standing varies a lot from country to country. As a general rule, however, the class ranking is white Hispanics on top, then mestizos and Creoles, then indigenous Amerindians and blacks at the bottom of the ladder. This is true except in West Indian Caribbean states, of course, where top government and business positions are held by blacks. In West Indian cultures, race is less important to class standing than wealth and family heritage.

Class rank is also determined by position of authority. In earlier times, Jesuit priests were near the top of class strata, but that has changed. Now military generals and high government officials rank about even at the top of the ladder. Business leaders come next, followed by urban workers, church leaders, and peasants. Of course in rural areas heavily populated by indigenous peasants, church leaders hold a much more elevated position.

Class rank is also determined by gender. In most underdeveloped countries and rural areas, elder men hold the top ranking, followed by young men, elder women, boys, and young women and girls. An older man holding a high military or government position, who also happens to be white (or mestizo or black in certain countries), is at the top of the ladder.

Do not interpret this ranking to mean that women cannot rise to the top of the class ladder. They most assuredly can and do. In Chile, Nicaragua, and Costa Rica, women hold key government jobs from legislator to president of the country. Women haven't made many inroads in the Latin business community, but that will happen in the future as well.

In most of Latin America, however, women do not enjoy the same class ranking or social status as men. This inferior social status of women, this gender gap, must change if these countries are ever to be accepted in the world community as civilized, modern-day nations and take their rightful places alongside Chile, Costa Rica, and Argentina.

Those are the basic heritage traits that over the years have determined to a large extent the primary culture of Latin America. However, to succeed in this region, you must also be cognizant of experiential traits that affect how and why Latin Americans do things they way they do. These traits vary a great deal from country to country and even within a country. Here are the experiential traits that I have found to be the most universal:

- Gender class difference
- The power of the church
- Racial bias
- National pride

Gender Class Difference

To first-time visitors, the Latin American gender gap, that is, the social status and attitudes that differentiate men and women, is probably the most obvious experiential trait. We saw in Chapter 3 that Costa Rica, Colombia, and Uruguay ranked one, two, and three, respectively, in the empowerment of women. Venezuela, Brazil, and Mexico were ranked at the bottom of the World Economic Forum's index. To ignore the cultural aspects of the gender gap is to disregard one of the most important differences between Latin American cultures and that of the United States.

Throughout Latin America, males have standards of behavior and expectations that are substantially different from those of females. The legendary macho man is very much in evidence. So is the equally legendary child-rearing female. The further down the social ladder you look, the more pronounced these differences appear. Conversely, the gender gap is much less obvious in the elite class.

From the perspective of foreign companies entering these markets, the significance of the gender gap will be felt in three ways:

1. In defining consumers
2. In defining the labor pool
3. In defining the community power base

Defining Consumers

According to reports released by the United Nations Economic Commission for Latin America and the Caribbean, nearly all able-bodied Latin American males earn income in one form or another, either in the formal economy or in the underground economy. But only one-third of Latinas earn any income at all. Even in the more developed economies of Argentina and Chile, women are less than 30 percent of the work force. In less-developed Guatemala and the Dominican Republic it's 16 percent and 17 percent, respectively. In comparison, U.S. women comprise about 41 percent of the work force.

These differences vividly depict the strong Latin leanings toward the traditional woman's role of raising and caring for the family. But there is another side to the story. Since 1990, political violence has brought many changes to several regions (most especially Peru, Bolivia, all of Central America, and Mexico.) An increasing number of women are now either supplementing family income by holding jobs or by engaging in entrepreneurial businesses. According to the World Bank, throughout Latin America, 33 percent of economically active people in urban areas are women. This compares to 45 percent in the United States. Unfortunately, these statistics leave out economically active citizens in rural areas, which account for a significant number of Latin Americans in less-developed countries such as Peru, Bolivia, Ecuador, and even parts of Mexico.

Although statistics are scarce, studies by the Center for Women's Business Research, the Inter-American Development Bank, and the World Bank indicate that a large proportion of rural women run their own micro-businesses. This is not from choice but from necessity. The male partners of these women have run off, have been killed, are missing, or are unemployed, and the women cannot find regular employment that produces enough income to sustain their families.

This is certainly an admirable approach to self-sufficiency. However, incomes are so meager that everything goes to buy essentials such as food and clothing—and not imported food and clothing. In fact, most women in rural communities, or at the lower end of the social scale in urban centers, couldn't possibly afford to buy imported goods of any type and therefore cannot be considered viable consumers of foreign-made products. Which brings us back to males. From a practical standpoint, if you are planning to export basic goods to these markets, you should aim your sales pitch at male consumers, with an accent on the value of your products to family members.

On the other hand, companies with product lines aimed at more affluent buyers will find a much broader customer base and little gender differentiation in terms of buying power. From Mexico to Argentina, an increasing number of daughters of the elite class are educated in U.S. or European prep schools and colleges. When these women return to their homeland, they have acquired the same tastes as Americans or Europeans and are avid shoppers. Consumer markets, like every other aspect of Latin life, must be viewed in light of class standing.

Labor Pool

The World Bank, the Inter-American Development Bank, and the United Nations Economic Commission on Latin America and the Caribbean studies referred to previously were mostly concerned with peasants in rural communities and lower-class areas of urban centers. When analysts studied employment and income, they looked at jobs in local companies as opposed to foreign-owned manufacturing plants. Clearly, this skewed the findings. In fact, foreign-owned companies are providing an increasing number of job opportunities for men and women alike.

Women and girls hold a preponderance of assembly-type jobs in foreign-owned plants, especially maquilas. Managers of both apparel and electronics assembly businesses prefer to employ women because of their skill and dexterity. Most men couldn't, or wouldn't, sew or handle a tiny soldering iron. And, as in other regions of the world, women will often work for lower wages than men.

Community Power Base

Although women are discriminated against in terms of wages and social standing, when it comes to the community power base, no one doubts that they are in charge. Men may be more visible, louder, and more demanding, but if you want to accomplish anything in a community, seek out the woman or women in charge. It's not hard to spot them. They generally have a flock of children, other women, and men around them. They exude authority. Recognizing and acknowledging this authority is extremely important when establishing an in-country factory, hotel, store, distribution center, or sales office. It's crucial if you plan to sell household products, such as vacuum cleaners, cosmetics, or dinnerware.

Regardless of government regulations concerning business licenses, labor laws, import clearances, and any other hurdle, if you get the community boss on your side, you stand a much better chance of success. Conversely, if the community (in the person of the woman or women in charge) does not want your facility in the neighborhood or believes your products to be detrimental to its families, you better look elsewhere. They will shut you out fast. That is what happened to the operations manager of a midsize U.S. clothing manufacturer.

This company operated several small assembly plants in free-trade zones in El Salvador and Guatemala. When it came to opening another factory in Honduras, local bureaucrats encouraged the company to choose a site away from free-trade zones, a site that the government wanted to get cleaned up. The company complied and opted for a location in a small, heavily populated area outside of San Pedro Sula. The property contained about a dozen ramshackle sheds that were homes for several extended families.

During the site survey, the operations manager noted a large woman sitting on a porch across the street from the buildings he was about to order demolished. She was the matriarch of the community, although the American didn't realize it at the time. After securing the required licenses and clearances from the local bureaucrats, he brought in a bulldozer, only to find more than 100 women camped outside the sheds. Regardless of his efforts, threats from local bureaucrats, and even a few soldiers summoned to clear the way, the women refused to leave. Eventually, the bedraggled American went looking for a different site, this time in a free-trade zone. He was quoted as saying that never again would he try to move into a Latin community without first clearing the way with the local matriarch.

Power of the Church

The influence of the church over the everyday lives of Latin Americans and the enormous impact it has on political, social, and business activities, puts dogmatic religious beliefs right up there with the gender gap as a prominent experiential trait. Every aspect of daily life, family values, entertainment (such as music, art, literature, the cinema, and athletics), conflict resolution, politics, motivation for economic improvement, travel preferences, and business matters is influenced by the church. For hundreds of years, when one spoke of the church in Latin America, by definition one meant the Roman Catholic Church. An estimated 450 million Catholics, almost half the church's global population, lived in Latin America.

But the power of the Catholic Church is fading fast. In at least a dozen countries, including Argentina, Chile, Honduras, and Peru, membership in the Catholic Church has dropped 10 to 25 percent in the past three decades. In 1970 Brazil, which had the largest congregation of Catholics in all of Latin America, 92 percent of the population claimed to be Catholic. In 1990, that had dropped to 84 percent. In 2000, of the 170 million people in the census, 74 percent claimed to be Catholic. To grasp the meaning of this decline as well as the importance of the modern-day church in Latin America, you have to understand its contradictions.

As was the case in most sixteenth-century conquests by European powers, missionaries swarmed over Latin America hard on the heels of Europe's conquering armies. Although most indigenous civilizations predated Europe by centuries, Spanish, Portuguese, French, and English priests considered these naked savages heathens. Building on a scaffolding of fear of the devil, fear of fire and brimstone, and fear of a hell for heathens, missionaries imbued these natives and the settlers who followed with values that to this day have not totally disappeared. Jesuit priests taught that the authority of the Supreme Being overshadowed that of mortal governments. Allegiances were to be formed with the Almighty, not with those mortals who ruled the land, although the official line was that these rulers were also divine representatives, along with the priests, of course.

For generations, priests stayed clear of politics. Then liberation theology took hold. This was a school of thought that found in the Gospel a call to free people from political, social, and material oppression. Liberation-minded priests turned the tables, focusing on social issues such as poverty, community development, and human rights, vociferously criticizing dictatorial rulers. Especially in outlying areas, the church became identified with social justice and structural change. During the 1980s, in Guatemala, El Salvador, and many regions in South America, liberation theology challenged the authority of military dictators and privileged one-party rulers. In the outlying areas of Central America, bishops and Jesuit priests alike became such thorns in the side of government troops that they were sought out and murdered along with guerrilla fighters.

When previously passive Jesuits morphed into vociferous human-rights advocates, teaching the primacy of divine authority over secular governments, those living in extreme poverty were the first to rise up in open rebellion against strong-arm military governments. But many people saw the folly of this. As a result, a vacuum existed for those who believed in the old-school teachings of acquiescence. In stepped Pentecostal fundamentalists from the United States. Underlying the Pentecostal theology is a belief that members should seek to be filled with the Holy Spirit in emulation of the apostles at Pentecost. Translated into daily life, this eternal search for salvation has given the poverty-stricken hope for a better tomorrow. Concentrating on the glorious hereafter, Pentecostal preachers teach the need to obey secular authority and to docilely accept the often cruel and inhumane conditions of this life.

The Pentecostal movement caught on like a wildfire, especially in areas dominated by abusive rulers, and has had a major impact on the relationship between governments and private sector businesses. By ceding secular authority to political leadership, whether elected or not, Pentecostal theology has become the right hand of those governments. This new, unquestioned power of officialdom has resulted in much stronger enforcement of government regulations, both with regard to the participation of foreign companies in local businesses and with regard to the acceptance of foreign imports in preference to locally produced products. If you plan to open facilities in countries or regions with strong Pentecostal leanings, you would be wise to research the impact that a downplaying of secular gains may have on worker productivity and efficiency.

While much lip service has been paid to raising the income of workers through better-paying jobs, Pentecostal followers are more attuned to non-monetary benefits, such as holidays, sick leave, personal time off, and so on. Also, pensions mean very little to people whose faith in their future well-being is based on the acceptance of divine providence.

Racial Bias

Latin American racial bias is partly inherited from the region's Hispanic background and partly a result of political, social, and economic events over the past hundred years or so. Racial bias manifests itself in several ways. Differences in skin color and cultural heritage seem to be the most prevalent. Guatemala is a good example of how the clash of cultures can bring about violent racial bias. The attacks that the government perpetrated on the Mayan Indians and their supporters in the 1980s and 1990s, primarily in the north, were at times as deadly as anything going on in the Middle East, Africa, or Eastern Europe. Murder and torture were commonplace. And why? The official line was that the military was merely trying to subdue guerrilla bands. However, the opinion of commentators from the front pages of the New York Times and many other U.S. publications, as well as officials from Amnesty International and other international watchdog organizations, was that the Guatemalan government was trying to wipe out the indigenous culture. Noted author and journalist Edward R. F. Sheehan, in his book *Agony in the Garden*, draws a similar conclusion. My observations of the region confirmed it to me. But why would the Guatemalan government want to eradicate the indigenous culture? Because over the years, not only in Guatemala but in other Central American countries as well, a strong racial prejudice against indigenous peoples has developed.

Such animosity toward a group of people descended from an advanced civilization that flourished centuries before the coming of Spanish soldiers is unwarranted. And when you consider that the majority of Central Americans are mestizos, that is, of mixed race, Hispanic and indigenous Amerindian, it does indeed seem strange that such racial prejudice exists. But it does.

Racial bias caused by cultural differences goes beyond indigenous groups. In Guyana and also in Trinidad and Tobago, unwarranted antagonism between West Indians and East Indians festers very prominently. In both countries, descendants of indentured laborers from India comprise about 50 percent of the population. Black West Indians, with scatterings of European descendants, make up the other half. Extreme racial hatred of one group by the other is the main reason for Guyana's soaring crime rate and Trinidad's rabid political confrontations. Both West Indians and East Indians tend to be somewhat antagonistic toward Americans, but mainly they are indifferent.

Although I have not seen the type of extreme prejudice against people with black skin that was prevalent in the United States fifty years ago, skin color is still a source of racial bias in Latin America. Fortunately, Latin Americans mostly hold such feelings in abeyance. On the other hand, you will find skin-color prejudice very prominent throughout the Caribbean. Except for Trinidad and Tobago and the Spanish-speaking islands, black West Indians run the Caribbean. Many have a strong racial prejudice against people with white skin.

I encountered open hostility against whites while working in Jamaica, Barbados, Grenada, and most prominently in the U.S. Virgin Islands. In other island states, racial prejudice against whites is covert, hidden from the naked eye, but there nevertheless. Of course, since tourism is the lifeblood of the Caribbean, casual visitors to the islands hardly ever see such prejudice.

You'll find less racial bias in the business community, but it has its share as well. It is evident in hiring practices, work assignments, pay scales, promotion opportunities, preferential licensing, import restrictions, tax collection, and in many other areas. You can't do much about racial bias except to recognize its existence when dealing with Latin bureaucrats, the military, customs people, and other authority figures.

Although today most Americans detest flagrant racism, you need to be very careful when setting up or managing a Latin American operation. On the one hand, it won't do to practice overt racism. Few Americans would voluntarily sanction company polices that treat employees, suppliers, and others who have dark skin or belong to indigenous groups any different than people of direct or mixed Hispanic heritage. Yet Americans must be careful not to violate local customs by ignoring race in our business practices. Although tricky, racial differences can be acknowledged without flagrant adherence to discrimination policies.

Americans must also be careful not to favor racially oppressed groups in an attempt to right a national wrong, as happened in the United States with federally mandated affirmative action laws. Maintaining a middle-of-the-road policy is the only sensible solution.

National Pride

National pride is very close to the surface for most Latin Americans. Notwithstanding the near chaotic conditions of several political, social, and economic institutions, Latins from every country in the region will defend the honor of their country against all comers. This has led to a form of nationalism as intense as anywhere in the world. It is the main reason that most logical groupings of nations have never been successful in forming cohesive common markets or free-trade pacts, even though doing so is probably the only feasible way to create a strong enough front to deal with the United States and other G8 countries.

The intensity of nationalism varies from country to country. Generally speaking, the larger the country or the more advanced its institutions are, the more prominent nationalism becomes. In any event, when visiting one of these countries, be sure not to make disparaging remarks about anything that could even remotely infringe on national pride. Doing so is a sure way to make enemies, land in jail, or get thrown out of the country. Remember that you are the guest. Honor local customs, including national pride, and you will likely be invited to return another day.

Chapter 6

Market Research: Performing a Country Survey

Whether you are a first-timer in Latin America or expanding into a new market, it makes sense to do as much market research as time and money allow. Such research should produce enough hard data to make intelligent marketing, financial, and manufacturing decisions and also to calculate a country risk assessment. Obviously, the more information you can pull together, the better chance you have of avoiding costly mistakes. You can get a fair amount of information without leaving home, such as a country's business structure requirements; audit, tax, legal, and licensing rules; potential communications bottlenecks; and the types of necessary insurance coverage.

On the other hand, reliable political and economic data, as well as market-specific information, can only be obtained within the host country. While several U.S. government agencies and Latin trade periodicals will give you a fairly good feel for current happenings in the political and economic spheres, to get the full scoop you need to see for yourself, and that means visiting the country. You'll have to go there to gather data on the following market-specific matters:

- Alternative advertising media
- Possible distribution channels
- Sales representative/distributor arrangements
- Business support activities (such as interpreters, safety and security features, banking, business permits, and informal trade barriers)

- Safety and security matters
- Exchange controls

Moreover, if your plans call for establishing a local manufacturing plant, distribution center, or sales office now or in the future, you'll need information about labor availability, sources of materials and supplies, inland transport, infrastructure conditions, and expatriate living arrangements.

You may have the personnel within your organization who could perform country surveys, but why bother with such a time-consuming task? Extensive interviews must be conducted with government officials, in-country managers of U.S. companies, potential customers, likely sales representatives and distributors, transportation executives, and various other individuals. It's usually more cost-effective to let a consultant separate the wheat from the chaff. I have performed any number of country surveys for clients in South and Central America, as well as the Caribbean. Plenty of well-qualified consultants can do the job for you. If you are interested in going this route, I suggest you start your search for one in Miami or Houston, where most are located.

If you do elect to use a consultant, the following rules of the road can save you a significant amount of money:

1. Describe to the consultant, in as precise terms as possible, exactly what you want and what your strategic objectives are for entering a given market.
2. Arm the consultant with as much data as possible about your company, its products, current markets, and personnel capabilities.
3. Ask the consultant to identify potential limitations on the scope of an assignment.
4. Find out precisely what research methodology the consultant plans to use and be sure you're comfortable with it.

5. Clearly define the level of detail you expect in each element of the survey.
6. Gather as much data as you can from U.S. sources first and turn over to the consultant the names, addresses, and telephone numbers of host-country referrals you have already uncovered. The less time spent in the field, the less the total cost will be.
7. Don't hesitate to have the consultant help analyze pre-research data. In the long run, the less time he spends in the field, the less the total cost will be to you.

Business Structure

If you are planning to export directly to end users or to intermediary distributors or trading companies that take immediate title to the goods, you don't have to worry about business-structure requirements. However, if you plan to initiate a joint venture or start up a local subsidiary, then the form and capitalization of the host-country business entity must meet the legal requirements of that country.

Some countries require import licenses that can only be granted to locally registered businesses. Others forbid foreigners from holding controlling interest in domestic companies. Foreigners may or may not be permitted to incorporate a business. You may have to operate out of a joint-venture partnership, possibly with the government as a partner. Some countries insist on hybrid business structures that combine the characteristics of partnerships and corporations.

The host country's embassy or trade representative office is the best place to get the rules governing business structure and ownership. While you're at it, pick up copies of any regulations that apply to import licenses, tax clearances, business licenses, foreign exchange permits, and other operating approvals.

Here are a series of questions about business structure and ownership that need to be answered:

- What laws relate to foreign business ownership?
- Is there a required business form? Corporation? Partnership? Hybrid?
- What are the restrictions on each form?
- Can or should tiered corporations be used?
- Do local laws require a host-country partner in a joint venture or other strategic alliance?
- If a local partner is required, what percentage of ownership must you give up?
- Must the joint venture carry one of the partners' names or can its name be completely divorced from them?

Audit, Tax, Legal, and Licensing Requirements

Many questions that relate to audit requirements, taxes, contract law, and licensing can only be answered by sources within the host country. You can get some information, however, from U.S. multinational accounting firms such as Ernst & Young, KPMG Peat Marwick, Pricewaterhouse-Coopers, and DTR International. Each of these firms publishes newsletters, special reports, and information pamphlets about broad changes in tax laws and reporting requirements. Each also prints booklets summarizing tax information for the use of individuals and corporations in every country in which the firm has offices. Be sure to ask for a directory of the firm's worldwide offices. It will contain the names and telephone numbers of resident partners, which can be invaluable information once you start your in-country research.

Every Latin American country has an embassy in the United States. Many also have trade promotion bureaus that stock a variety of booklets and pamphlets describing audit and tax laws and import licensing regulations. You should be able to get the following questions answered from either a country's embassy or its trade promotion office:

- What are the financial reporting requirements, and when do financial reports have to be filed?

- Must these reports be verified by an in-country registered audit firm, or can that be done by your U.S. auditors?
- Will audited consolidated financial statements from your parent company suffice, or must the in-country entity be audited separately?
- Has a Tax Information Exchange Agreement been executed with the United States?
- What are the tax rates?
- What income is included or excluded for corporate and individual tax purposes?
- Is a tax levied on imports or direct sales?
- Are there any tax incentives applied to foreign direct investments?
- Are intracompany transactions with your U.S. parent taxed?
- Is there a withholding tax on repatriated earnings or royalties?

Economic reforms have created very fluid legal systems in all Latin American countries. Laws governing contracts, taxes, the protection of intellectual property rights, business permits and licenses, pensions, workers' security, and a host of other topics continue to change. And one country's laws are significantly different from another's. Moreover, the court systems in many countries are virtually inoperative. Cases take an inordinate amount of time to come to trial. The following questions need to be answered:

- What are the laws governing business permits, import licensing, and work visas?
- What ethical problems, if any, might arise in dealing with host-country correspondents?
- What are the incorporation or business structure laws?
- Are there any restrictions or requirements for setting up joint ventures or partnerships with local firms?

- What unique features of the host-country's litigation laws pertain to American firms doing business there?
- What liability do U.S. exporters have for actions taken by in-country representatives that may be in violation of the Foreign Corrupt Practices Act or other laws?
- Which legal counsel, in the United States or in the host country, will review sales, countertrade, or other contracts?
- Are laws that protect intellectual property rights enforced?
- Who will handle arbitration cases if they arise?
- Do you have Washington contacts that can cut through red tape when you apply for federal assistance?

Communications Bottlenecks

I can't think of anything more frustrating for managers trying to communicate with customers, sales representatives, distributors, or their own facilities than to find that telephones lines are down, electricity is out, and mail delivery takes four weeks. Although conditions are improving in Argentina and Chile, the rest of South America, Central America, parts of Mexico, and the less-developed Caribbean islands continue to live with grossly inferior communications infrastructures. These facilities are gradually being updated throughout the region, but they still have a long way to go to meet modern-day demands. Meanwhile, the business community must get along with systems that are antiquated, unreliable, and very costly, including unreliable postal systems, or use e-mail, which is about the only feasible way to communicate quickly, provided you and the recipient both have electricity.

International mail service to and from major cities has improved a lot in recent years, but in-country service to remote regions is still abysmal. So is service throughout Central America. On more than one occasion, local mail handlers have opened mail, confiscated the contents, and intentionally lost the envelope or package. If you must send a package or a sheaf of documents, use an international courier.

However, even with reputable couriers such as DHL and Federal Express, problems can arise. A couple of years ago, I sent a bundle of documents to Guyana. The package arrived in about seven days, all right. But it had obviously been opened and resealed, which, of course, DHL denied. Fortunately, the package contained only documents that were useless to anyone other than my client, so no damage was done.

When gathering information about potential communications bottlenecks, it's a good idea to put what you are told to the test. More often than not, the official line about telephone service, couriers, and electronic mail is vastly different from actual practice. Start by asking the following questions:

- Does the country's telephone service operate on direct dialing for international calls?
- If not, can local operators (hopefully English-speaking) place international calls?
- Can overseas calls be placed and received on private lines, or must a central telephone office be used?
- How much do international calls to and from the United States cost?
- Can U.S. credit cards be used to place calls from the host country?
- Is telex used extensively?
- How practical are cell phones for local calls and for international calls?
- Is fax service reliable? How much does it cost?
- Is Voice over Internet Protocol (VoIP) a viable alternative?
- How reliable is the electric power system?
- Is it practical to use computers? How does the local weather affect their performance? Are backup generators readily available?
- Are computer repair facilities and parts available?

- How reliable is the local postal service, and what does it cost to send mail between the United States and the host country?
- What is the mail delivery time to and from the United States?
- Do major courier services deliver close to the offices of your sales representative or to your distributor's facility? How long does delivery take with DHL or FedEx?

Insurance

In the United States, people assume that they can get insurance coverage for virtually anything merely by calling an insurance broker. This is certainly not the case in Latin America, where the insurance industry is in its infancy. Many types of coverage that Americans are accustomed to are either unavailable or grossly inadequate. Although group health insurance programs may include overseas coverage, many do not. Popular Blue Cross/Blue Shield policies or HMO plans, for example, generally exclude hospital or physician charges incurred while out of the United States. If your insurance carrier excludes international care and will not write separate riders, specialized international healthcare bureaus are a good alternative. Be sure to select one that writes policies that include emergency transport back to the States. This is essential in the event of serious illness or accident.

I have found that two of the best travel insurance carriers are Travel Assistance International, P.O. Box 668, Millersville, MD 21108, (800) 821-2828, and International SOS Assistance, Inc., 3600 Horizon Blvd., Suite 300, Philadelphia, PA 19053, (215) 942-8000. Policies issued by these two carriers always include air transport back to the United States in an emergency.

Some types of limited insurance coverage may be available within the host country. However, until very recently, most insurance companies have been state-owned, so don't expect the breadth of coverage or claim service that U.S. carriers offer. Argentina, Chile, and a few others have taken steps to privatize employee benefit programs, group health and life insurance, and non-health insurance companies. Compared to U.S. carriers, however, Latin insurance companies are very small. On the plus side, foreign firms are occasionally permitted to form joint ventures with local insurance companies. Check it out.

Although privatized insurance companies and joint ventures with U.S. carriers offer limited opportunities for buying insurance locally, you will be ahead in the long run by arranging coverage through a U.S. carrier. That way you'll avoid any possibility of not getting adequate insurance at a reasonable cost.

In addition to health insurance, it's a good idea to review coverage for losses caused by work-related accidents, damage to or disappearance of ocean shipments, destruction of property, product liability, vehicular accidents (especially with rental cars), and government expropriation of your property. Except in rare circumstances, the types and amounts of coverage we have in the United States are not available in Latin America, although this is changing. Workman's compensation for offshore employees is not available anywhere. Several marine insurance companies cover damage or loss of goods during ocean shipping. If you have trouble locating one, check with your state insurance commission. Property insurers are a different story. AIG is the largest carrier in this business. Lloyd's and CIGNA also insure offshore property. If you plan to have an in-country facility, however, the federal government's Overseas Private Investment Corporation (OPIC) is hard to beat.

Although a much larger organization than OPIC, the UN's Multilateral Investment Guarantee Agency (MIGA) provides guarantees that serve as insurance policies to cover risks of currency transfer, expropriation, war and civil disturbance, and breach of contract by host-country governments. This is a must if you expect to have in-country facilities.

Most Latin American insurance companies have never heard of product liability coverage. To offset this shortfall, a few U.S. carriers grudgingly cover claims from a U.S. company's Latin customers. Also, since many Latin markets are beginning to open to foreign investment, your U.S. carrier may already sell policies for local coverage through a subsidiary or a joint venture with a host-country carrier. Can't hurt to ask.

Your company fleet policy may or may not cover rented or leased automobiles in Latin America, although several U.S. insurers do. Since automobile rental insurance is usually several times more expensive when purchased in country, it's always a good idea to make sure you are covered before leaving home.

That's about all you can do from the States. The rest of your survey will have to be conducted within the host country. It should focus on political and economic conditions, general business conditions, transportation options, security issues, personnel matters, and exchange controls. Obviously, the amount of information and the time involved in gathering everything depends on how much you can get from U.S. sources and the extent of your planned involvement within the country.

If you plan to have an in-country presence, you'll need information about labor conditions, local transportation, and probably expatriate living conditions. If such a presence involves manufacturing, it will be essential to get information about the availability of materials or components, the extent of government subsidies, and the current status of infrastructure development. If your market strategies are limited to exporting, the survey can be restricted to a review of market conditions, such as competition, distribution options, advertising media, and so on. Research procedures described in the rest of this chapter cover the waterfront and assume full involvement with an in-country presence.

Political and Economic Environment

Since Latin American market strategies must be long term to be effective, it doesn't make much sense to invest money and time in a country that is politically unstable or has a shaky economic future. It's prudent to make sure that the market will not only be accessible over a reasonably long period but that it will be growing. Although certainty is a rare commodity in any Latin American country, by putting together as many specific facts and sound opinions as possible about a country's future potential, you should be able to reduce the risk of unrealistic growth projections.

Aside from international trade periodicals and U.S. government agencies focused on trade and foreign direct investment, some of which provide excellent coverage of Latin America, the most reliable and current information about political and economic conditions will come from the host-country offices of the American Chamber of Commerce, multinational banks, multinational accounting and consulting firms, and in-country subsidiaries or divisions of other American companies. The following questions should be asked of representatives from each organization:

- Does more than one political party vie for office?
- What are the views of each toward continuing economic reforms?
- When is the next election? What is the prognosis?
- Is the current government favorably or unfavorably disposed toward Americans and especially toward American imports?
- What is the country's current relationship with the U.S. government?
- What other American companies are doing business in the country?
- What is the official attitude toward foreign direct investment, especially from U.S. companies? What is the unofficial attitude?

- What does the country's main economic base consist of? Imports? Exports? Locally produced goods and services?
- Are statistics available to show economic growth or decline (for example, gross domestic product, interest rates, inflation rates, annual capital expenditures, imports, exports, wage rates, unemployment rates)? If so, what are they, and how reliable are they?
- What are the country's demographic trends (for example, age spread, income distribution, geographic dispersion, and so on)?
- Are major businesses owned or controlled by the government?
- If so, is there a privatization program under way and how many major businesses are being sold?
- How strong are local business cartels?
- What specific trade barriers hinder foreign imports or foreign investment? Licensing? Exchange controls? Protected industries?
- Do government regulations restrict the distribution of imported products?

Market-Specific Business Conditions

If you are planning to do your own marketing, as opposed to working through a trading company, the first step is to build a local sales organization. Here are the main questions to focus on:

- What government regulations restrict the scope of in-country sales personnel?
- What regulations govern contractual relationships with sales representatives?
- Can sales representatives also distribute their own or competitors' products? Can distributors also sell retail? Do the same import licensing regulations apply to sales representatives, distribution centers, and end-users?

- Does the government encourage countertrade arrangements? If yes, what incentives or restrictions apply?
- Do trading companies handle imported goods? If yes, is this the dominant form of foreign sales representation?

Although much of this information can be obtained from government sources, the enforcement of official regulations should be confirmed with local merchants, producers, and sales representatives. The opinions of managers of in-country subsidiaries of American companies are usually reliable. If anyone knows the ins and outs of local business, these people do, and most are more than willing to show a compatriot the ropes. Also, if practical, try to get the opinions of sales representatives, distributors, and end-users that import products. Their answers won't always be straightforward or necessarily reliable, but if you plan to use in-country representatives, find out now what regulatory obstacles you'll run into.

In much of South and Central America, certain industries are controlled by cartels or firms linked through a tight web of cross-holdings. Colombia probably has more business cartels than any other Latin American country. Constraints imposed by these cartels can be devastating. Government officials won't admit to such informal barriers, but they do exist, nonetheless. If it looks as though cartels have control of your markets, it may be best to look into the prospects of doing business in another country.

The same type of good ol' boy network that pervades the U.S. defense, petroleum, and pharmaceutical industries is very evident in parts of South and Central America and throughout the entire Caribbean, stretching across a wide range of industries. Personal relationships among sales representatives, bankers, bureaucrats, lawyers, and accountants create a steady crosscurrent of preferential treatment and favors. Try to identify such power brokers early in the game so that appropriate groundwork can be laid to smooth the way through customs, bank relations, government regulations, and grievance settlements. This can usually be accomplished surreptitiously with no one the wiser. First, ask government officials and sales representatives for referrals to bankers, lawyers, and accountants (under the guise of needing to engage these professionals for other matters). If Citibank, Chase, BankBoston, or another American bank has branch offices in the country, or if a multinational accounting firm such as Ernst & Young or PricewaterhouseCoopers has a presence there, these organizations should be the ones recommended to you. Any other referrals would be suspect. Second, ask bankers, lawyers, and accountants for referrals to bureaucrats and sales representatives. Although it is more difficult to sort out relationships going this direction, referrals from U.S.-affiliated banks, consultants, lawyers, and accountants will be as straightforward as possible under the circumstances.

Competition

Business cartels also have a direct bearing on the severity of local competition and hence on pricing. Very seldom can imports compete on price with locally produced goods of similar quality, technology, or style. Cartels have even been known to block the sale of imported goods that have higher technology, better quality, or flashier styles. The fate of personal computers in Brazil in the early 1990s is a good example. For years, Brazilian computer manufacturers continued to make the same low-quality products with little new technology. The computer cartel was powerful enough to get the Brazilian government to impose stringent import controls over foreign-made computers, so that higher-technology products from IBM, Apple, and other U.S. companies were virtually shut out. Eventually U.S. firms broke through by forming joint ventures with local manufacturers. However, local companies still retained majority ownership in many of these joint ventures.

Multinational companies with local manufacturing plants may also pose a serious threat. Your market research should be extensive enough to uncover the names of competitors, along with their estimated market shares, growth prospects, and product development plans. Although this type of information is probably the most difficult of all to come by, the local American Chamber of Commerce office is a good place to start. Also, U.S. Commercial Service personnel at American embassies maintain extensive files on local companies. Interviews with potential competitors will quickly reveal the extent of their product lines as well as pricing structures.

If your competition comes mainly from other American, European, or Asian companies, and such competition is firmly entrenched, it may pay you to join forces with one of these companies in some form of alliance, either a joint venture or some other business structure. Two importers working together may be able to capture a larger market share than either could do separately.

Advertising and Sales Promotion

You can count on the fact that your U.S. advertising and sales promotion tactics will not be effective anywhere in Latin America, with the possible exception of a few Caribbean islands. Demographics, cultural norms, infrastructure deficiencies, and a variety of other conditions make it necessary to design promotional schemes that recognize subtle preferences unique to each market. To find out what form of advertising works best for your products, you may want to test a few approaches. Or you may be lucky and find that research alone gives you the answers.

Pure observation can also be invaluable. For instance, an aircraft parts manufacturer initiated an export program to Chile and planned to use the same television spots that had proven effective in American markets. I was asked to produce comparative analyses of the effectiveness of Chilean television, radio, newspaper, and direct mail advertising. Unfortunately, statistical data was very meager. During my visits to Santiago, as well as to Valparaíso to the north and to the Talcahuano/Concepción region to the south, I observed that radio, newspapers, and billboards apparently reached a wide segment of the population. Having verified these observations with the Chilean-American Chamber of Commerce in Santiago and the managers of several Santiago-based branches of American and European companies, I relayed these findings to my client. The company dropped any thoughts of television commercials and hired a Chilean agency to produce radio spots and a series of billboard displays.

Government Subsidies

Most Latin governments offer direct subsidies of one type or another as incentives to attract foreign investment and trade. The form of subsidy varies, but most can be grouped as follows:

- Reimbursements for labor training costs
- Exemption from income and other taxes, often for periods of ten years or more
- Low-interest, long-term financing
- Exemption from import customs duties
- Rent-free housing for foreign managers

Although some subsidies are part of publicly announced economic reforms that can be researched from the States, less obvious ones must be uncovered during an in-country investigation. Usually a visit to the country's ministry of finance will reveal the government's entire incentive package.

Some incentives are not granted to foreigners across the board but must be negotiated on a case-by-case basis. My experience has been that negotiating anything with government bureaucrats is a nightmare. Better results will probably be forthcoming if you let a local attorney with government connections make the arrangements. You may even be able to get your incentives without ever sitting down at a negotiating table.

American Chamber of Commerce offices, U.S. embassies, or American companies with a presence in the country won't be much help in obtaining special government handouts or exemptions. The exception, of course, is if the government views your product as critical to the country's well-being. In that case, government officials will likely play up to embassy officers and other U.S. bureaucrats in hopes of retaining the goodwill of Washington. However, even then, I have never had much direct help from U.S. embassy personnel. These folks can point you in the right direction, but they can't overtly help you with business matters. Embassy officers will, however, brief you on the current status of government-to-government relationships.

Transport, Licenses, Security, and Labor

Such matters as alternatives for inland shipping, import licenses, recommended security measures, sources of raw materials, and the availability and cost of labor and management personnel need to be researched in-country if you plan to have a local production or distribution facility. Are materials, supplies, and production equipment available locally, or will they have to be imported from the United States or other countries? If importing is necessary, are import licenses or permits required, and how do you get them?

Information about licenses or other formal import barriers needs to ferreted out from government agencies. As for unofficial barriers, trading companies are the best sources of information. Subsidiaries of American companies are also reliable sources of information, especially if they have imported similar materials or equipment of their own. Managers of both types of businesses are usually willing to point out who must be paid off to get your materials and equipment moved from the dock to your plant or distribution center. Furthermore, if materials, components, or equipment are to be sourced in-country but from a location far removed from your facility, managers of these companies can also fill you in on alternative modes of transport and the cost of getting the equipment or materials to your plant.

The safekeeping of company property is a problem in any Latin American country, just as it is in the United States. I suggest you make arrangements for enclosing any company facility with a ten-foot-high metal fence topped with barbed wire. Most likely, you will also need to hire twenty-four-hour guard service. Be sure to make such arrangements while you're in-country doing the survey. By the time equipment, vehicles, and other company property begin to arrive, it may be too late. Better to be safe than sorry.

To get the scoop on labor regulations, stop in at the ministry of labor and any other government department that administers workers' rights and benefits laws. Get a copy of pertinent labor laws and at the same time find out which jobs are covered under collective bargaining agreements. Nearly all Latin American skilled and unskilled workers are unionized. That means a stop at the union hall nearest your plant or warehouse. Check out the rules governing hourly wage rates, vacation and holiday schedules, special benefit packages, and other labor-related information. Try to get a feel for the availability of the particular skills needed in your facility. It may be necessary to recruit workers through labor brokers or to negotiate labor contracts through a local law firm, in which case you should be sure to get the names and addresses of both.

Poke around the docks to learn about problems you will likely encounter at the port of entry. Customs personnel will tell you about off-loading procedures as well as duties to be paid.

Payoffs will probably be necessary. Local trading companies are the best source of information on that. Ask about the amount of such payments and to whom and when they should be paid. If materials or equipment must be transported overland, be sure to find out about tariff rates, the availability of trucking lines, and on-loading and off-loading requirements from any contract hauler.

Infrastructures and Free-Trade Zones

Your main infrastructure concerns will probably focus on the quality of roads and rail lines, perhaps seaports and airports, and the availability and reliability of telephone service, electricity, and water supplies. Take the matter of roads. Typical questions you should resolve include these:

- Do toll roads connect your new facility with markets, suppliers, and ports of entry? If so, what are the tolls?
- Are roadways paved?
- How well are roadways, bridges, and tunnels maintained?
- Can company-leased trucks pass over bridges and through tunnels safely?
- What is the danger of roadway bandits?

Local subsidiaries of American or other foreign companies that truck over these same roads are the best sources of information. Be sure to ask about the status of roads currently under construction and whether they will impact the delivery of materials and equipment or affect outgoing shipments. It's also a good idea to verify the accessibility and cost of freight forwarders, containerization, and on-loading facilities if you plan to export from the country.

To get a fix on the availability and reliability of utilities, check with American Chamber of Commerce officials and local businesses. A short survey of businesses in the immediate area of your planned facility will quickly reveal any utility problems that can be expected. The chamber office will provide an historical perspective on recent conditions that have affected a broader area.

Many countries have free-trade zones. These zones are specific areas set aside by the government for duty-free storage of imported goods to be transshipped out of the country or, in some cases, converted to finished products by assembly or other operations. Try to get answers to the following questions about these zones:

- Where are free-trade zones located?
- What facilities are available within the zones? What are the rental costs?
- What support activities—labor recruiting, bookkeeping, transport, utilities, and so on—are available in the zones? What do these services cost?
- What types of goods can be moved through the zones?
- What type of work (if any) can be performed on the goods held in the zones?
- What restrictions are there on the destination of shipments out of the zones (for example, sales to domestic markets, exports to specific countries, worldwide exports, and so on)?

If you or any of your people plans to carry samples into a country, you need to know which ones are duty-free and which are taxed. Import duties as well as extensive customs procedures can be avoided by obtaining an ATA (Admission Temporaire) Carnet. The ATA Carnet is a standardized international customs document used to obtain duty-free temporary admission of certain goods into countries that are signatories to the ATA Convention. Under the ATA Convention, commercial and professional travelers may take commercial samples, tools of the trade, and advertising material as well as cinematographic, audio-visual, medical, scientific, or other professional equipment into member countries temporarily without paying customs duties or taxes or posting a bond at the border of each country visited. Applications for carnets can be made to Corporation for International Business, Harris Bank Blvd., 325 North Hough Street, Second Floor, Barrington, IL 60010. Unfortunately, not all Latin American countries accept ATA carnets. Chile was the first to do so in October 2005, and other countries are following suit. I suggest you check the Corporation for International Business Web site listed in Appendix F for countries added since that date.

Personnel Matters

If your marketing people are not fluent in Spanish or Portuguese (for Brazil) be sure to interview two or three interpreters recommended by an American branch bank or the American Chamber of Commerce office. Then contract with the one who shows the best perception of negotiating techniques and speaks the most fluent English.

Language errors are the most common mistakes made by newcomers to Latin America. For instance, the sales manager of a U.S. computer parts manufacturer made her first trip to Brazil and quickly found out that a smattering of Spanish was not enough, certainly not in Brazil. Confident that two years of college Spanish would get her through, she was aghast when, upon returning the States, she asked the local Berlitz office to translate from Portuguese into English the sales contract she had signed. She had negotiated the right price, but for three times the quantity of parts she had intended.

Ensuring the safety of personnel, either traveling to Latin America or relocating there, is an important consideration but one all too often overlooked. As soon as you arrive in a country, make three contacts as soon as possible:

1. **American embassy:** Let the embassy know exactly where you will be staying, for how long, and whom to contact in the United States should an emergency occur. Don't expect any business help from embassy officials, and don't expect them to resolve your disputes with local government bureaucrats. However, in a genuine emergency (such as a coup d'etat or natural disaster), the American embassy may be the only place to get help, and embassy officers are anxious to give it.

2. **American Chamber of Commerce:** The local office can be extremely helpful in less serious emergencies. Officials always know who the power players are in the police department and government agencies. When push comes to shove, they will always try to help an American in distress. Tell your people to give the chamber office the same personal data given to the embassy.

3. **Local police department:** Let the police know who you are, why you are in their country, where you are staying, and whom to contact in the event of an emergency. Be sure to include both local contacts and those in the United States.

The best sources of emergency help may well be other expatriates, mainly other American, Canadian, or British expatriates. In addition to the American embassy, the American Chamber of Commerce, and the local police, get to know the names and telephone numbers of expatriates in key business and banking positions. I have never known an American, Canadian, or British expat to shy away from helping a compatriot in need.

During all my travels around the globe, I have learned one trick that has benefited me more than any other. I always carry on my person two typed letters, one in English and one in the local language and dialect, containing my name, U.S. address and telephone number, local address and telephone number, passport number, where I'm staying, special medication I take and what I am allergic to, my blood type, and the names and addresses of at least three local people to contact in an emergency. To prevent theft, I always carry the letter in a pouch fastened to my body inside my shirt.

If your plans call for personnel to be traveling extensively or living in a country, gather as much information as possible about the cost and availability of accommodations, the cost and availability of local transportation (both public transport and private automobiles), educational facilities, and the names and telephone numbers of as many American or English-speaking expatriates living in the country as possible.

Exchange Controls

What if you couldn't repatriate earned income, couldn't transfer working capital funds into the country, or didn't have access to these funds once they were deposited in a local bank? Wouldn't that be a disaster? Better take the time now to find out about laws relating to currency exchange and repatriation of profits and capital, then make arrangements for the secure movement of your company's money both in and out of the country. At the same time, open an account at a U.S. branch bank, arrange for the conversion of U.S. dollars into local currency, and get assurances that you will have access to this currency for paying bills.

When applying for permits to move or convert funds, be sure to arrange for business licenses, labor-hiring clearances, tax identification numbers, and any other permits necessary to conduct business in the country.

Summary

We have covered a lot of data in this chapter. Following the check lists provided will enable you to do a complete market research survey. But don't assume that these are the only steps to take. Special situations require special research. Here's a summary of which items to check out or obtain:

- Government restrictions that prevent the use of U.S. employees as in-country sales personnel
- Regulations controlling contractual relationships with local sales representatives
- Regulations governing sales representatives and distributors
- Local government's position on countertrade arrangements
- Names and addresses of local trading companies that import U.S. products
- Relative strength of business cartels
- Reference checks on important government bureaucrats and local sales representatives from banks, lawyers, and public accountants

- Names and market shares of local and multinational competitors
- Description of directly competing products and names and addresses of manufacturers and distributors
- Advantages of forming alliances with competing U.S. exporters
- Advertising and sales promotion options
- Relevant government incentives or subsidies, those that apply across the board as well as those that must be negotiated
- Availability and cost of skilled and unskilled labor
- Information about formal and informal barriers to the import of materials and production equipment
- Local sources of materials and supplies
- Current condition of port facilities and inland transport alternatives
- Reliability of electricity, water supplies, and telephone service
- Location, availability, and restrictions related to free-trade zones
- Availability of security guards and property fencing
- Legal requirements for currency conversion and repatriation of earnings and capital

In addition, the following steps need to be taken:

- Open bank accounts with U.S. branch banks
- Make applications for business license, labor hiring clearances, tax identification number, and any other required permits
- Interview two or three interpreters and contract with the best one
- Test out potential personnel safety hazards
- Create safety/security checklist for company personnel
- Apply for carnets

Chapter 7

Country Risk Assessment

Which country offers the least risk and greatest profit potential? Which market-entry strategy will yield the highest return on investment? These are key questions that must be answered prior to proceeding with any Latin American marketing plan. But even before analyzing country risk and market-entry options, you need to carefully define your objectives relative to international trade. Are you limited to exporting so that a direct investment in a Latin American country never enters the picture? Or would you consider an in-country facility such as a manufacturing plant, a distribution center, or a sales and customer-service operation?

By considering alternative market-entry strategies, you can weigh one against the other. For instance, you might prefer to serve Latin American markets solely by exporting directly from a U.S. plant or warehouse. But perhaps that country's Byzantine customs procedures, high tariffs, or outlandish taxes would make your imported products noncompetitive with locally produced goods. In that case, you might reach markets more effectively from an in-country factory or warehouse. Such a facility could then produce products for local consumption as well as for export to other countries. But that may not work, either. Regulatory and legal bottlenecks may make such a direct investment inappropriate. Or perhaps you have personal reasons for not even considering a Latin American facility, and the pendulum swings back to exporting from the United States. Perhaps the solution is a combination of exporting and direct investment.

If your business is a profession, financial services, communications, or other service industry, you could offer your services either from your U.S.-based office or from an in-country presence. By opting for the latter, you might be able to provide services to customers or clients in other Latin American countries from this same office.

If you are in a manufacturing business, how about producing parts or components or sourcing raw materials from a Latin American location for use in your U.S. factory or to stock your U.S. warehouse? The savings in labor costs could then be passed along in lower prices to make your products even more competitive in U.S. markets. Maquiladoras along the Mexican border have been doing this for many years.

Once you define your company's objectives, you can begin to evaluate the inherent risks of doing business in a given country. The best way to identify country risks and to judge the efficacy of market-entry strategies is to conduct a country survey. With a firm understanding of the country risks you will face and your various market-entry options, you can perform a country risk assessment and devise strategies that will yield the highest return at the lowest risk.

Country Risks

Country risks are those political, economic, and social conditions that you have no control over. You cannot exert any influence over them, and you cannot change the underlying factors that create these risks. They are external to your span of authority, and they are present in every country. Yet in the long run, these country risks, or external risks as they are commonly called, will determine the success or failure of your strategic marketing decisions as much as or more than your company's management policies.

Political instability is one external risk that can disrupt the best-laid plans. Consider, for example, Venezuela. A short time after President Hugo Chavez took office, new laws were enacted that revoked civil liberties and encouraged police intrusion in businesses and personal lives. This resulted in unwarranted arrests and confinement for hundreds of people. Businesses closed. Foreign investment dried up. And many foreign companies withdrew completely from Venezuela. Another case of how a duly elected Latin president can throw a monkey wrench into the best-laid plans occurred when President Evo Morales Aima of Bolivia nationalized the nation's natural gas companies and later de-nationalized them because his government lacked financial resources to operate them. You can't plan for this type of contingency. However, you can attach a probability of occurrence to political instability and factor that into your country risk assessment.

Financial upheaval is another external risk that manifests itself from time to time in every Latin American country. Take the case of Argentina in 2002. Faced with a default on the country's international debt obligations, Interim President Eduardo Duhalde dumped the nation's currency board, threw out the peso's ten-year-old one-to-one peg to the dollar, and created a financial nightmare of massive currency devaluation and climbing inflation.

In addition to political instability and financial upheaval, a host of other external risks impact market-entry strategies. Corruption, inflation, functional illiteracy, and several other conditions will unquestionably affect how successful you are in profitably marketing your products or services. A careful analysis of these risks will help you choose the market-entry strategy that best meets your objectives.

Defining Market-Entry Options and Risks External to a Company's Authority

Doing business in Latin America has never been straightforward. New risks seem to crop up every day to muddy the waters. These risks must be balanced against available market-entry options. Under most circumstances, the greater the risk you're willing to take, the greater your profit will be. Nevertheless, entering a high-risk market could result in significant losses. To compensate, you may have to develop one or more market strategies beyond those you originally conceived.

One way to determine the relative merits of alternative market strategies is to quantify the probable impact of external risks on these strategies through a country risk assessment. Before proceeding, I should clarify three assumptions that underlie such an analysis:

1. Any risk assessment is valid only when one country is compared with another country (or countries) within a homogeneous region. For our purposes, I have defined three homogeneous regions: South America, Central America, and the Caribbean. The case study used later in this chapter to demonstrate the concept of risk assessment deals only with South America. However, the same principles apply to Central America and the Caribbean.
2. The analysis of strategic benefits must be considered over a span of years. I prefer to use five years, although this may be too long a span for some companies.
3. By definition, all economic analyses are judgmental. In other words, the person preparing the analysis adds his or her biased judgment to the statistical facts.

To begin, we must define two criteria: the types of external risks—political, economic, and social—that, to differing degrees, are present in all Latin American markets and the principal market-entry options available to your business. Looking at external risks first, those that have the most influence on strategic market-entry decisions seem to be caused by the following:

- Political instability
- Government interference
- Corruption
- Street crime

- Inequality of income distribution that can lead to social upheaval
- Inferior education systems that result in functional illiteracy
- Infrastructure deficiencies
- High inflation rates
- Exchange controls as part of an inefficient banking systems

When analyzing the impact of these external risks, look at how they affect each market-entry option. Some companies have only one market-entry option: exporting. Most U.S. companies, however, should at least consider three market-entry scenarios:

1. Exporting products or services from the United States to a Latin American country
2. Establishing an in-country presence to produce goods or services for local markets
3. Exporting products or services from an in-country presence to other Latin American, European, or Asian countries

Offshore sourcing of parts, components, or sub-assemblies at maquila plants could be a fourth strategy. Obviously, all four options may be used alone or in tandem to develop any number of long- and short-term market-entry alternatives. The next step is to quantify the impact external risks have on your choice of marketing, direct investment, and sourcing strategies.

Quantifying the Impact of External Risks

Economists, statisticians, and government agencies have all developed models that purport to quantify external risks and their relevance to business strategies. Some models can be helpful, while others are merely a play on numbers. However, they all have three common characteristics:

1. They are difficult for businesspeople to use.
2. They rely on broad-based and often outdated data.
3. The mathematics employed by each can produce radically different answers.

I have found through extensive research and more than forty years of doing business in Latin America that evaluating the magnitude and impact of rapidly changing risks and opportunities can best be done by applying informed judgments to relatively unsophisticated models without the use of complex mathematical compilations.

To illustrate the type of conceptual thinking involved in country-risk assessments, I'll use a case study of one of my consulting clients, a mid-size manufacturing and distribution company in the electronics industry named U.S. Fabrisource and Avionics Corporation (USFAC). I was hired by this company to help develop a meaningful index that could be applied to the evaluation of external risks and market-entry options. Here is the model we came up with.

A Case Study: U.S. Fabrisource and Avionics Corporation

Looking for new markets that had potential for expanded growth in both their consumer and industrial product lines, top management at USFAC determined that several South American countries looked promising, provided an intelligent assessment could be made of the potential medium-term risks involved. Management also decided that the most viable market-entry options were twofold: exporting from the United States, and establishing a production or distribution facility within one or more South American countries. In addition, the president wanted to investigate the possibility of sourcing certain components from one or more countries.

A team of marketing, production, and finance people was formed to carry out a country survey for all South American countries except Suriname and Guyana. Upon completion of its research, the team agreed that the previously described nine external risks did, in fact, apply to all countries. For each country, the team then assigned factors of zero to ten to each of the risks and to the four market-entry options. **Table 7-1** shows the scoring system that was used.

Table 7-1 | Scoring Risks and Market-Entry Options

Risk	Market-Entry Options
10 = no risk	10 = sure bet
9 = extremely low risk	9 = extremely high benefits
8 = very low risk	8 = very high benefits
7 = low risk	7 = high benefits
6 = below average risk	6 = above average benefits
5 = average risk	5 = average benefits
4 = above average risk	4 = below average benefits
3 = moderately high risk	3 = moderately low benefits
2 = very high risk	2 = very low benefits
1 = extremely high risk	1 = virtually no benefits
0 = stay out of here	0 = no benefits

The next step was to determine how serious each of the nine risks was relative to USFAC's market objectives. For simplicity, the research team used a scale of one to five, with five being the most serious risk and one being the least serious. The team decided that political instability and social upheaval would be the most disruptive to USFAC's strategic plans and warranted a seriousness factor of five. An inefficient banking system was judged to be of virtually no risk to the company and was assigned a factor of one.

Obviously, the seriousness of political instability, corruption, functional illiteracy, or any external risk varies for every company. In other words, you must determine the seriousness of each risk relative to your business.

With a quantified evaluation of each risk in hand and a factor assigned to represent the relative seriousness of each risk, the USFAC team then calculated a weighted average of risks for each country. This was done by multiplying each risk factor (zero through ten) by the appropriate seriousness factor (one through five). The results were then totaled and the sum divided by nine (the number of external risks considered in the analysis).

This process was repeated for the four strategic market-entry options. Each market-entry option was assigned a benefit factor of zero to ten and was then weighted on a one-to-five scale, with five being the option that the team believed would result in the greatest benefit to USFAC and one assigned to that option deemed to be the least beneficial. The team then calculated a weighted average for each option. The results were totaled, and the sum was divided by four (the number of options considered) to arrive at a single market-entry option factor. The final step was to add the weighted average of risks to the weighted average of strategic market-entry options to arrive at a risk assessment factor for each country. **Table 7-2** shows the results this model produced.

Table 7-2 | Risk Assessment Analysis

Potential Risks	Argentina	Brazil	Chile	Colombia	Venezuela
Political instability (5)*	7	6	8	4	3
Government interference (3)*	6	3	8	3	2
Corruption (4)*	5	2	5	3	3
Street crime (2)*	6	2	5	2	3
Income distribution/social upheaval (5)*	5	3	5	6	2
Functional illiteracy (2)*	4	3	8	6	8

Infrastructure deficiencies (3)*	7	5	4	4	6
High inflation rates (3)*	8	5	7	2	2
Inefficient banking systems (1)*	8	7	9	8	5
Weighted average potential risks	19.0	12.1	19.7	12.6	10.4

Strategic Market-Entry Options

Exporting to (5)†	9	7	7	6	8
Local satellite plants (2)†	2	3	1	5	4
Produce for local markets (4)†	8	8	8	3	7
Exporting from (2)†	9	8	9	8	9
Weighted average market-entry options	24.8	22.0	21.8	17.0	23.5
Risk assessment factor	43.8	34.4	41.4	29.6	33.9

Potential Risks	Bolivia	Ecuador	Paraguay	Peru	Uruguay
Political instability (5)*	5	3	2	3	5
Government interference (3)*	5	2	2	2	5
Corruption (4)*	5	4	3	2	5
Street crime (2)*	5	3	5	1	5
Income distribution/social upheaval (5)*	3	6	3	4	8
Functional illiteracy (2)*	3	5	4	3	8
Infrastructure deficiencies (3)*	3	2	3	2	6
High inflation rates (3)*	5	1	3	1	3
Inefficient banking systems (1)*	4	2	2	6	8
Weighted average potential risks	13.2	10.4	9.0	8.0	17.9

Strategic Market-Entry Options

Exporting to (5)†	7	7	2	5	5
Local satellite plants (2)†	0	0	0	0	0
Produce for local markets (4)†	5	4	1	8	6
Exporting from (2)†	2	7	4	5	7
Weighted average market-entry options	14.8	16.3	5.5	16.8	15.8
Risk assessment factor	28.0	26.7	14.5	24.8	33.6

* = *Seriousness of risk—5 equals greatest harm*

† = *Benefits of market-entry decision—5 equals greatest benefit [ETB]*

Table 7-3 summarizes the results of this model-building exercise.

Table 7-3 | Risk Assessment Summary

	Risk Assessment Factor	Weighted Average Potential Risks	Weighted Average Market-Entry Options
Argentina	43.8	19.0	24.8
Chile	41.4	19.7	21.8
Brazil	34.4	12.1	22.3
Venezuela	33.9	10.4	23.5
Uruguay	33.6	17.9	15.8
Colombia	29.6	12.6	17.0
Bolivia	28.0	13.2	14.8
Ecuador	26.7	10.4	16.3
Peru	24.8	8.0	16.8
Paraguay	14.5	9.0	5.5

As can be seen, specific risks as well as potential benefits from different market-entry strategies varied widely among countries. In Argentina, for example, with a risk assessment factor of 43.8, the nine external risks would impact USFAC's profitability and return on investment of the four market-entry options less than in any other South American country. But because external country risks and the benefits from alternative market-entry strategies do not necessarily go hand in hand, the USFAC team recognized that it was necessary to look at both sides of the fence, risks and benefits.

In the case of Argentina, the weighted average potential risk factor of 19 showed that risks were greater than in Chile (which had a factor of 19.7). However, the weighted average market-entry options factor of 24.8 was also greater than Chile's 21.8. At the other end of the spectrum, analyses of conditions in Paraguay indicated that regardless of which market-entry strategy USFAC chose, the negative impact of external risks would be greater than in any other country.

The results of Brazil's risk assessment presented another interesting case. Brazil's combined risk factor of 34.4 placed it as the third least-risk country in the region. Yet its weighted average of risks alone, 12.1, placed it as the sixth least-risk country. (Five other countries earned lower weighted average risk ratings.) As an offset, Brazil's weighted average of market-entry options of 22.3 placed it third after Argentina and Venezuela.

This demonstrates the importance of looking at the potential benefits that may be derived from alternative market-entry strategies as well as the probable impact external risks may have on these strategies. Looking at risks alone won't do the job. It also shows that risk assessment for a single country is meaningless. Scores for all countries under consideration must be compared.

The biggest advantage in the model we built for USFAC is its simplicity. Anyone can use it. You don't have to be a mathematician or a statistician to benefit from it. I have used this model countless times for my own businesses and for clients. It's not very scientific, but it does force you to look at many market conditions you might otherwise miss.

By using the results of your market research to assess the desirability of each market-entry option and by applying your expert judgment to determine the severity of the nine external risks, you should be able to develop market-entry strategies for countries that will yield the greatest return at the least risk. But it's important to remember that any risk-assessment model will yield useful results only in direct proportion to the accuracy of the data used and the experienced judgment of the preparer.

Many country risk-assessment models are available. There is nothing magical about which one to choose. Some are very helpful. Others are a waste of time. As an alternative, you could develop your own model. If you like to work with standard deviations and probability theory, or if you like to plot logarithm graphs, then by all means use statistical models that employ these tools. As long as the results of the calculation make sense relative to what you have learned from your market research, the analysis should be helpful in making strategic marketing decisions.

Spend the time to look at as many models as you can. Create your own model. Talk to other people in your industry who have ventured into Latin America, and ask about the difficulties they have encountered as well as the benefits they have derived from their choice of country and market-entry strategy. And by all means, spend sufficient time and resources preparing your market research so that you know exactly what obstacles you are likely to encounter.

The main idea in any country risk assessment is to consider for any potential market as many hazards and opportunities as time and resources permit. A reasonably meaningful end result is the most important element of any analysis, not the tools used to get there.

Chapter 8

Marketing Channels

To sell products in U.S. markets you must solicit potential customers; structure competitive pricing; reflect societal values and customs in your product's workmanship quality, utility, and perhaps style; warrant your product's performance; and, depending on the product, offer customer training, parts replacement, or other customer service features. These same features hold true for Latin American markets.

But Latin American markets inject additional factors that impact your marketing efforts. You will definitely need a local presence of some type, either in-country sales representatives, distributors, or a partner. You will have to allow extra time for making the sale and for collecting your money. Add in language hurdles and cultural barriers, and you get a significantly more complicated mix.

Five marketing channels can be used to reach Latin American customers. All five effectively recognize these special factors. Two channels use indirect selling methods, while three are direct:

1. **Indirect-marketing channels**
   - Selling to U.S.-based commissioned agents of Latin American governments and companies, Latin American export management companies, or foreign export trading companies, all of which represent Latin American end users
   - Selling to intermediaries, such as U.S. export management companies and export trading companies, who then export on their own account

2. Direct-marketing channels
  • Selling through your own captive export trading company
  • Selling through Latin American sales representatives, trading companies, or distributors
  • Selling directly to Latin American customers, either with company sales personnel or alliance partners

The capabilities of your export sales department, your company's financial resources, and the level of management interest in international trade determine whether an indirect or a direct channel is most appropriate. I should add, however, that the majority of companies just starting an export program find it easier and less expensive to go the indirect route. The easiest and least expensive way is to sell to Latin American commissioned agents.

Commissioned Agents of Latin American Governments and Companies

A growing number of foreign commissioned agents roam the United States looking for products that cannot be purchased in their clients' countries. In many cases, these agents represent Latin American governments that need goods and services for infrastructure projects, for military arsenals, or for state-owned manufacturing, retailing, or service (primarily financial services) businesses. They also represent the private sector, buying consumer products for Latin American retail chains or materials and components for Latin American manufacturers. It's fairly easy to make contact with both public and private sector buyers through Latin American embassies, Latin American trade promotion bureaus, U.S. government agencies, or trade shows.

There is nothing mysterious about selling to Latin American commissioned agents. Customer promotions, terms and conditions of sale, packaging, shipping protocol, and credit and collection procedures are the same as those used when selling to domestic customers in Los Angeles, Dallas, Tulsa, or Mobile. In fact, accountants record these sales as domestic sales, not as export sales.

Commissioned agents may not be the best way to get established in a Latin market, however. It might make more sense to use export management companies. These independent sales organizations are the least complicated method of selling export products.

Export Management Companies

Before finalizing your export strategies, I suggest you ask yourself the following questions:

- Do I have the financial resources to staff an export department with qualified sales personnel?
- Do I know how and where to find Latin American customers for my products?
- Am I confident that I can quickly master the intricacies of dealing with customs officials, in-country transport companies, and Latin sales representatives or partners?
- Do I have the time to devote to learning the various nuances of export markets?

If your answer is no to even one of these questions, then you should seriously consider hiring an export management company. More than 5,000 small and mid-size American companies, and a few very large ones, already use these organizations.

Export management companies, or EMCs, are a convenient indirect outlet for American-made goods. In some cases, EMCs act like manufacturers' representatives, serving as the selling arm, or export sales department, for several manufacturers of non-competing products, soliciting orders and transacting business in the name of the various producers they represent. In other cases, EMCs serve as your very own export sales department, working exclusively for your company. These Latin American sales experts may be paid retainers, commissions, or a combination of retainers and commissions. A third option is for an EMC to purchase goods directly from manufacturers and then resell them overseas for its own account. Some combine the three approaches. A few of the bigger EMCs with substantial resources will even help finance export orders. Most EMCs are quite small, however, and do not engage in trade finance.

EMCs maintain their own Latin American networks of sales reps and distributors. This puts them in a solid position to develop market strategies for U.S. clients, to arrange for shipping and customs documentation, to purchase foreign risk and marine insurance coverage, and, in some cases, to help arrange supplier or buyer credit. As a seller, you don't incur any credit risks, shipping costs, overseas selling expenses, or customer service costs. In fact, you won't even know the identity of your customers.

If your company is unwilling or unable to support its own export sales department, using an EMC is a clean way to increase sales without adding risk. However, the price for such a luxury is steep. Since EMCs on retainer earn their profits when they resell the goods offshore, they must buy those goods at prices significantly lower than market prices, generally at product cost plus a small mark-up.

EMCs may also operate as commissioned sales representatives. In that case, your company retains title to the goods until customers accept shipments. This is less expensive than paying a retainer, but you bear all financing costs, credit risks, and carrying charges, plus storage costs of inventory stocked at the EMC's distribution warehouses.

Despite these drawbacks, EMCs are an effective way for smaller companies to test the waters of export markets without incurring the costs of full-blown international sales departments. They are very popular and have been around for a long time. You can get a list of EMCs from the Federation of International Trade Associations' Web-based directory. (See Appendix F.) If EMCs don't make sense for you, perhaps you should consider export trading companies.

Export Trading Companies

The U.S. Congress passed the Export Trading Company Act in 1982. This act permitted the formation of export trading companies (ETCs) by groups of competitors without fear of antitrust action. The avowed purpose of this legislation was to increase the competitiveness of U.S. companies by allowing them to market products jointly, just as Dutch, Japanese, and British companies have done for decades. The Export Trading Company Act also permitted bank holding companies to form ETCs. The theory was that by allowing banks to engage in commercial, non-banking transactions, they would be more receptive to requests for trade finance, thereby encouraging more American companies to export. (This theory was never proved. Nine out of ten commercial banks still shy away from anything having to do with international trade.)

After passage of the act, individuals, companies, trade associations, states, and cities jumped in. Enamored by the presumed success of giant Japanese trading companies, Americans were eager to partake in the vast profits offered by global trade. Unfortunately, few actually took the time to understand the intricacies of international trade, and ETCs failed as fast as they were formed.

My favorite anecdote about ETCs relates to a used-car salesman from Keokuk, Iowa, who married a lady whose family came from Paraguay. Tempted by the possibility of tapping his in-laws for local sales contacts, he quit his job, incorporated himself as an ETC, packed his bag for a four-day stay, and took off for Asunción, expecting to land several orders for whatever anyone wanted to buy. Upon landing, he was asked by his in-laws what product lines he represented. His response typified the naiveté of the new traders: "Any product you want. I'm going to get the order first and then source out a supplier back in the States." Today he is back in Iowa, selling used cars.

ETCs usually take title to a U.S. manufacturer's products and then export them for the ETC's own account. They function independently, more or less as a sales middleman, sourcing U.S. products from a variety of manufacturers to meet the needs of known Latin American clients. Typically, an ETC performs a sourcing, or wholesale, function between buyer and seller and does not assume any responsibility to either party in the transaction.

A few ETCs refuse to carry inventory or perform after-the-sale customer service. These companies operate strictly as commissioned agents, charging the seller or the buyer a percentage of the export value. Most export trading companies, however, do just the opposite. They buy everything from manufactured goods to raw materials (at 10 to 15 percent below wholesale price) from a variety of U.S. manufacturers then resell them for their own account. Your trade association is the best source for locating an ETC to fit your needs.

Whether you opt to sell to Latin American commissioned agents, choose to use an EMC, or go with an ETC, indirect selling methods impose some disadvantages you would not encounter when using your own export sales department to sell directly to Latin distributors or other private sector Latin buyers, or to Latin American governments. Here are some of the drawbacks that come with indirect selling:

- Your personnel will not learn the complexities of exporting for future expansion to other Latin American markets.
- You will find that some Latin American buyers are reluctant to deal with a third party.
- Through EMCs or ETCs you have no control over defining your customers, setting selling prices, designing promotions, or handling after-sale service.
- EMCs and ETCs will always concentrate on those products that bring them the most profit, shunning new product offerings or those products with limited potential.
- The majority of EMCs and many ETCs are small businesses with limited financial resources available to stock your products or offer trade finance.

Furthermore, although U.S.-based Latin American com-missioned agents, EMCs, and ETCs all offer convenient, low-cost ways to increase sales without becoming involved in complex international trade transactions, indirect selling is not a viable long-term growth strategy. Intermediaries are just that—intermediaries. Brand loyalty is very hard to establish through intermediaries. Relying on intermediaries will never gain you market prominence, nor will it establish your com-pany's reputation as a quality supplier. In the end, a long-term stake in Latin American markets cannot be proxied.

As you have probably discerned from the foregoing dis-cussion, the distinction between ETCs and EMCs is often blurred. It's hard to tell one from the other. However, ETCs usually handle products from many manufacturers and sell to a single customer or a select group of customers. EMCs, on the other hand, normally handle products from a single manufacturer and sell in the open market.

Captive Export Trading Companies

Setting up your own captive export trading company (CETC) may be a better way to go. With a CETC, you avoid the loss in margin that occurs when selling to independent ETCs or through EMCs. Moreover, by marketing products for other exporters, the trading company you set up in, say, Caracas or São Paulo will bring in extra profits. One of my favorite CETC cases involved a long-time client, Washington Com-puter Corporation of America, otherwise known as WCCA.

WCCA manufactured PC computers and peripheral hardware. The CEO was interested in both Venezuelan and Colombian markets but felt his company could only tackle one country at a time. He ordered his staff to proceed with country surveys and country risk assessments for both countries. The results indicated that a significant market existed in Colombia for WCCA's PC line. The company proceeded to form a joint venture with a Colombian distributor and hired two Spanish-speaking sales managers for its export sales department.

Before turning the Colombian partner loose, however, the CEO and his staff developed a strategic marketing simulation model to determine the impact of various forms of Colombian competition, demographic trends, import regulations and other customs peculiarities; the role of certain influential government officials; and a distribution option for Bogotá and Cali.

By asking "what if" questions and varying their assumptions, the group evaluated the influence of each factor on the company's export program. They concluded that Colombian markets could be penetrated much faster and broader with a CETC. WCCA formed a CETC in conjunction with an export program and located its main office in Bogotá with a branch office in Barranquilla. The result? In the first two years, WCCA exceeded its Colombian sales forecast by 300 percent. It also picked up a whole new business, marketing computer peripherals for other U.S. firms through its trading company.

A typical CETC will take title to export goods and handle all export operations independent of its parent company. The CETC may handle one product line or multiple lines. It may export to one country or trade worldwide. Furthermore, CETCs can be formed with partners from banks, other manufacturers, state and city agencies, trade groups, or service organizations. These passive partners often provide working capital funds while the company that originates the CETC handles all management and administrative duties. With the CETC assuming all trading risks, your parent company can concentrate fully on other operating matters.

If you decide to form a CETC with other companies, banks, or government agencies, don't forget to apply immediately for a Certificate of Review. This certificate is a legal document issued by the U.S. Department of Commerce with the concurrence of the U.S. Department of Justice that provides antitrust protection for the export activities specified in the document. In other words, this certificate makes it perfectly legal to collude with other companies in the formation and operation of a CETC.

If you are interested in exploring the possibilities of forming a CETC, the U.S. Office of Export Trading Company Affairs lays out the requirements and advantages in a booklet titled *The Export Trading Company Guidebook*. This office also sponsors seminars and regional conferences on various aspects of the Export Trading Company Act. You can order the booklet or get additional information from Export Trading Company Affairs, Room 7021, U.S. Department of Commerce, International Trade Administration, Washington, D.C. 20230.

Foreign Trading Companies

Exporters from Japan, Great Britain, the Netherlands, and several other trading nations found long ago that trading companies could market and distribute products more efficiently on a global scale than any single producer could. More recently, exporting companies from non-traditional trading nations such as Argentina and Brazil have learned the same lesson. It's safe to say that today, trading companies have become the principal form of marketing worldwide. In Latin America, major trading companies operate in all the large metropolitan markets.

Foreign trading companies are as different from U.S. export trading companies as night is from day. The only similarity is the designation *trading company*. Many Japanese, Dutch, British, and German trading companies are huge conglomerates with marketing, financial, and distribution arms that permit a truly global reach. The Japanese trading companies Mitsui, Komatsu, Mitsubishi, and Sumitomo have been active for years in Chile, Peru, Colombia, and Brazil. German and Portuguese trading companies compete fiercely in Brazil. British trading companies are active in Argentina and are increasing their presence in Venezuela. A few American corporations formed joint-venture trading companies with foreign partners. Some trading companies handle specific product lines for small or mid-size companies. The easiest way to make contact with foreign trading companies active in your markets is through that country's trade development bureau.

Direct Selling

To remain competitive, sooner or later you'll have to set up your own international marketing organization, either with sales managers who monitor Latin American distributors out of your home office or through a network of sales personnel stationed in key sub-markets throughout the region. Dumping exporting activities on your domestic marketing organization can be a big mistake. Nine times out of ten it will not work. The selling, distribution, and administrative activities related to exporting are so much more complex and time-consuming than comparable domestic functions that a separation of duties is the only efficient way to operate.

Structuring an Export Sales Department Organization

Your export sales group should have offices apart from your domestic sales department, if possible in a separate facility. It should report directly to your top marketing executive. As export sales grow, along with the number of export sales personnel, reporting lines should shift to a high-level administrative officer. Companies with substantial export sales often find it convenient to centralize all direct and support functions in a separate international division. If your company exports two or more different product lines, or plans to attack more than one major market, it might be advantageous to organize a separate export sales group for each product line or market right off the bat.

It's interesting to note that in a recent survey, the majority of CEOs of companies that had exported successfully for a long time felt that their success resulted more from a proficient sales force and the methods used to sell and distribute their products than from any unique or superior product attributes.

Sales Representatives

After setting up an export sales organization, the next step is to determine how to distribute your products. Latin American sales representation varies significantly from country to country, depending on the cultural and legal peculiarities of each market. All countries, however, have representative laws substantially different from those of the United States. The peculiarities of Venezuelan laws exemplify the types of situations you will run into.

In Venezuela, actual market conditions and business protocol are seldom as advertised. Corrupt customs officials, arrogant bureaucrats, unfathomable trade laws, and cagey hustlers pretending to be import agents can all too easily frustrate newcomers. One broadly reported instance involved difficulties with sight draft payments. Venezuelan buyers either delayed or refused to claim merchandise from the receiving port. Customs officials then impounded the products, the U.S. shipper was charged large fines, and the goods were sold at auction. To complete the circle, the agents to whom the goods were originally shipped purchased the goods at severely discounted auction prices. Since Venezuelan laws do not require an importing company to pay its bank before obtaining the original documents necessary to get the merchandise transferred out of customs, customs officials may release the goods to anyone who presents a copy of the bill of lading and posts a bond for duties.

Wrongful transfer of goods at the port of entry is certainly not restricted to Venezuela. Abuses of various types have been reported at several other Latin American ports. It pays to check references for sales representatives and distributors before you agree to any type of contractual arrangement in any Latin American country.

When Is a Sales Representative Your Representative?

Murky distinctions between forms of representation, including the separation between sales representatives and customers, have caused confusion for more than one U.S. exporter. For example, a local company can act as a manufacturer's representative, import-distributor, dealer, wholesaler, and retailer—all at the same time. The same company that acts as a sales representative, taking orders on commission, may maintain inventory for distribution to other companies and also operate a retail store. Many retailers who import directly from exporters also buy through sales agents, jobbers, and dealers. Returning to Venezuela for a moment, that country does not issue import licenses. Neither does it publish lists of importers. According to Venezuelan law, anyone can import, making it very difficult to find out who is actually doing the buying. Fortunately, except for large department stores, Venezuela has practically no general merchandise importers, and rarely do agents or distributors take on competing lines. Under President Hugo Chavez, Venezuelan market conditions and business laws are undergoing dramatic changes, however, so if you're interested in this country, continue to verify shifts in representative regulations and other commercial laws.

Loose definitions of sales representatives, distributors, agents, and customers are not restricted to Venezuela. Each country has its own commercial laws. Virtually no two are alike. When exporting to any Latin American market, it makes sense to clarify these laws during your country survey.

Confusing Laws

In addition to agency and representation laws, other provisions in a country's commercial code affect the way agreements with representatives or distributors are written. Most countries require that, to be valid, contracts must be written in that country's language, use metric measurements, state all monetary values in local currency, be signed by an attorney, and be notarized. Although a few Latin American governments have not yet enacted contract laws for representatives or distributors, even those laws that have been enacted are seldom enforced. This means that when a contract is canceled, indemnification clauses are difficult to invoke. Moreover, companies that choose to carry Latin American representatives or distributors on their payroll must abide by labor laws that frequently entitle employees to profit sharing, bonuses, pension payments, and separation allowances.

Laws that regulate sales to government agencies are another matter entirely. With little or no uniformity, compliance requirements must be researched case by case. If you plan to sell to government agencies or state-owned businesses, be sure to obtain all licenses and permits necessary to conduct business in the country, and register your company with appropriate government bureaus. This is a prerequisite to getting on the right bidder's lists.

Distributors

As with agency and representation laws, regulations affecting both the definition and actions of distributors vary country by country. Typically, Latin American distributors are merchants who purchase American-produced goods at substantial discounts then resell them at a profit. In addition, distributors frequently provide after-the-sale customer service, offer product repair facilities, and stock spare parts inventories. It is not unusual for them to carry non-competitive but complementary product lines.

Distributors provide valuable services that could not be offered, or could only be offered at great expense, by U.S. exporters. For example, as residents of the host country, distributors know the characteristics of local markets. They offer advice about customs regulations, pricing strategies, distribution peculiarities, and customer expectations. Competent distributors also handle customer complaints and questions about technical product applications. Furthermore, since distributors are not bound by the restrictions of the Foreign Corrupt Practices Act and other legislation that hampers U.S. companies, they are more competitive with European and Asian firms.

Some companies set up training programs for their Latin American distributors to be certain that they know the technical aspects of a product. Others stock parts and materials at the distributor's warehouse for repair and maintenance work. Regardless of the specific relationship, it is crucial to put contractual terms in writing in order to avoid future misunderstandings about what you want your distributor to do and how it will be compensated.

Chapter 9

Advertising

The Latin American advertising industry is in its infancy. According to ZenithOptimedia, an advertising research firm, of the $406 billion spent on advertising worldwide during 2005, Latin America accounted for a measly $18 billion, or 4.4 percent of the total. Even Africa and the Middle East reported more advertising expenditures, at $21 billion. Brazil and Mexico were the big Latin spenders, accounting for 35 percent and 19 percent of the total $18 billion, respectively. Next in line were Colombia (7 percent of the total $18 billion), Argentina (6.2 percent), Chile (3.5 percent), Venezuela (3.1 percent), and Panama (1.3 percent.) All other Latin America countries together accounted for about one-fourth of the total expenditures. Nevertheless, it's hard to build brand recognition anywhere in Latin America without engaging in some form of advertising. From a media perspective, Internet advertising is the fastest growing mass media and might be your most effective, least-expensive way to go in Brazil, Mexico, and Argentina. Internet advertising is also coming on strong in Colombia's metropolitan areas. Later in this chapter, we'll take a look at the future of Internet advertising throughout the region.

Anyone who has done business in Latin America and studied the format and content of prominent advertising approaches can vouch for the marked differences from those seen in the United States. These differences are partly due to the deep chasm between Latin American mores and cultural traits on one hand and those of the United States on the other hand. They are partly a result of European, African, and Asian influences. And they are partly caused by turbulent external market forces—political, social, and economic. These external market forces have by far the biggest impact on your choice of advertising media, copy content, design layout, and market coverage.

Successful choices of media, copy content, and design layout also differ markedly among Latin American countries and even among regions within countries. Television commercials used in Brazil will not be effective in Argentina. Advertisements in Mendoza newspapers will not do well in Buenos Aires dailies. Effective ads in Jamaica will not reach a like audience in Trinidad and Tobago. Each country, and in many cases each sub-market within that country, has unique customs and infrastructures that materially affect how and where advertising will bring the best results.

It goes without saying that effective advertising campaigns must be tailored to the market demands of each class of customer. Extreme variations in language styles, consumer tastes, literacy rates, infrastructure development, and environmental factors make standardization in Latin America impossible. Although the broad guidelines discussed in this chapter can point the way, specific advertising campaigns must be designed to fit each unique market.

Take, for example, the matter of literacy. Universal schooling through secondary grades has, over the years, brought adult literacy rates in the United States, Europe, and Japan up to the 85 to 95 percent level. Most people can and do read newspapers and magazines, at least occasionally. Since these periodicals reach broad markets, they are an excellent medium for advertising many consumer products.

On the other hand, literacy rates are much lower in Latin America and vary widely among countries. Since fewer than 25 percent of Latin American school-age children complete secondary education, reading comprehension and vocabulary standards are far below those of the United States, Europe, or Japan. In a large country like Brazil, the percentage of literate people changes from one section of the country to another section and from urban metropolises to remote villages. A population of 186 million is scattered over a landmass as large as the continental United States. Many Brazilians live hundreds of miles from schools. Illiteracy in these regions clearly impacts the official statistics. Overall, no one knows the literacy rate for Brazil's entire population. Nevertheless, using U.S. standards as a basis for comparison, estimates place the overall adult literacy rate at 50 to 60 percent for the approximately 100 million Brazilians who live in larger towns and cities.

Infrastructure development, especially the availability of electric power and telephones, also has a major impact on the choice of advertising media. If television sets are a scarce commodity, TV commercials won't reach many consumers. On the other hand, because radios are very common all over the region, advertising in that media can be counted on to hit a much broader market than television, newspapers, or magazines.

Many made-in-America products are very popular in Latin America because they are deemed to be of superior technology, design, style, or utility. As long as products are perceived to have quality workmanship and are readily available, customers will pay slightly higher prices for American-made goods and wait slightly longer for delivery, in much the same way that in the past many Americans used to go this extra step to acquire perceived high-quality Japanese electronics and German automobiles.

But there is another side. Intense national pride can easily turn customers away from imported products in favor of those made locally. This not-made-here attitude is especially prevalent in nations that have a large entrepreneurial business base, such as Colombia, Brazil, and Mexico. Although this phenomenon affects consumer goods more than capital goods, on the whole it impacts all industries in which local producers compete with the quality and utility of imports. If your product lines compete head-on with strong local producers, you will do better by downplaying the made-in-America image and slant your advertising copy toward local pride.

A good example of how this can be accomplished occurred when a client, Hormast Sporting Goods, first broached Brazilian markets in Natal and Fortaleza with its line of high-quality hammocks. Instead of exporting direct to local retail outlets, Hormast set up a warehousing operation in the Manaus free-trade zone. Workers were hired to add a crocheted frill to the hammocks and repackage them in containers similar to those used for domestic hammocks. Advertising copy carefully emphasized that although the hammocks were made to an American design, they were produced in Brazil. Hormast's initial advertising campaign was so successful in establishing brand loyalty that within a year, the company began exporting hammocks directly from the United States to Brazilian distributors.

Cultural Sensitivity

Avoid culturally sensitive jargon like the plague. As American markets become more and more competitive, advertising agencies regularly invent new words and phrases to describe a product's features and benefits. Meaningless adjectives, misplaced nouns, double entendres, and clichés all aim at attracting the American consumer's eye. TV, newspaper, and magazine advertisements all use them. If you try these catchy words and phrases in Latin America, no one will understand your message. Viewers might enjoy a cartoon character prancing around or appreciate seeing a pretty girl demonstrate a product, but they will never grasp the message you are trying to convey.

And stay away from idioms and slang words. You can be sure that they convey an entirely different meaning when translated into Spanish or Portuguese. A classic faux pas oft-quoted in advertising courses at U.S. universities was committed by the Parker Pen Company more than thirty years ago. It advertised its famous ball-point pen as the Jotter, but in Latin America, *jotter* translates to *jockstrap*. Before committing your advertising expenditures, it only makes sense to be sure that the copy will be correctly understood by the customers you are trying to reach.

Also, be aware that many Spanish words used in say Mexico or the Dominican Republic have an entirely different meaning in Argentina, where the Spanish language is heavily influenced by the large number of European immigrants attracted to its shores. This influence has created a type of jargon that gives many words a sexual innuendo. Here are some classic examples from my friend Frank Yanni, recently retired vice president of Wyeth Pharmaceutical Company who lived in Buenos Aires for many years:

- In Mexico, the verb *coger* means to hold, to grab onto. In Argentina it is used to describe a sexual act.
- In Mexico, the noun *concha* describes a shell, as in marine life. In Argentina, it translates as vagina.
- In Mexico, the noun *bicho* refers to all types of bugs and insects. In Argentina, it connotes a man's penis.

The only way to avoid making a very serious error in your advertising copy is to hire a translator from the country in which your ad will run to validate the message you are trying to convey. Before committing your advertising expenditures, it only makes sense to be sure that your message says what you really mean it to say. No one intentionally offends customers. Yet, many words and phrases used in U.S. advertisements have entirely different, and often offensive, meanings in Latin America.

The same holds true for the use of color in your advertisements. Red, purple, orange, black, and so on do not have any important significance in the American culture, but they may be very offensive in Latin societies. In Brazil, for example, the color purple is usually interpreted as the color of death.

Alternative Media

Advertising can take many forms, depending on market breadth, types of products, and budgets. The most popular methods for reaching a wide audience include television or radio commercials, the cinema, newspapers (daily and weekly), magazines (popular and trade), billboards, posters, telephone directories and, in Brazil and Mexico, the Internet. More focused markets can be reached at much less cost through the use of commercial envelope fly-leaves, circulars or flyers, matchbooks, holiday greeting cards, engraved pencils and pens, calendars, or newsletters. However, demographics, infrastructure, and local customs may significantly reduce your number of choices in any given market.

Direct marketing in any form is still in its infancy. Unreliable mail service, low rates of telephone penetration, and inefficient transportation systems severely limit exposure. Furthermore, lists of potential customers, whether by address or by telephone number, are usually not available. Those that can be found tend to be of poor quality or are closely controlled by their preparers, making it impossible to know the buying characteristics of mail or telephone-call recipients. An as-yet sparse use of credit cards in less-developed countries presents additional challenges. Accessibility to potential customers varies significantly, depending on whether the markets are rural or urban. If you decide to use customer lists of any type, take the time to build your own database, even if that means beginning with a very small one. One way to begin, at least for the direct marketing of commercial and industrial products, is to collect names and addresses from advertisements in trade journals. Participation in trade shows and conferences will also net a small list of potential buyers for both consumer and commercial products.

Consumer-product companies often find that flyers left in stores, beauty parlors, lobbies of movie theaters, and ticket offices of sporting events bring good results. Properly designed brochures left in such locations can also help build a database.

Bus posters (with tear-off coupons) reach a fairly large audience, as do roadside billboards. Although many countries are beginning to have a high penetration of television sets, nearly everyone already has access to radios. Moreover, cinemas are popular in urban areas throughout the region. Print media, such as magazines and newspapers, have caught on in a few countries where literacy rates are climbing.

All media are vastly underdeveloped throughout Latin America, and wide differences exist among countries. As one would expect, you can get your message across easier in more developed countries such as Argentina, Uruguay, Mexico, and Costa Rica than in less-developed nations like Paraguay, Bolivia, Peru, and Nicaragua. **Table 9-1** shows the breakdown of the percentage of the population of each country that has access to major media.

Table 9-1 | Percentage of Population with Access to Advertising Media

Country	TV Sets	Radios	Telephones	Newspapers
Argentina	29	68	20	4
Bolivia	12	68	7	6
Brazil	33	43	21	4
Chile	24	35	21	10
Colombia	28	54	18	5
Costa Rica	23	77	30	9
Dominican Republic	10	18	10	3
Ecuador	21	41	12	10
El Salvador	19	18	11	3
Guatemala	6	8	7	3
Guyana	7	47	10	8
Honduras	10	41	5	6

Jamaica	19	80	15	6
Mexico	27	33	2	9
Nicaragua	7	27	3	3
Panama	19	30	13	6
Paraguay	21	18	5	4
Peru	15	27	6	9
Trinidad and Tobago	34	53	33	12
Uruguay	53	60	32	24
Venezuela	19	30	11	21
United States	84	211	61	21

Source: CIA Factbook, 2006; World Almanac 2006

Table 9-1 clearly identifies the vast differences in media coverage. Take TV, for example. In the United States, 84 percent of the population has access to TV. But at the top of the Latin American scale, only 53 percent of Uruguay's population has access to TV. This means that advertising on Uruguay TV could reach about half the population. That's not bad for Latin America. On the other hand, you certainly would not waste money on TV ads in Guatemala, where only 6 percent of the population watches TV. Well, maybe that's not so. After all, statistics seldom tell the whole story. More than 40 percent of Guatemala's population lives in Mayan villages in the remote North. These folks do not have any TV. Since that skews the statistics, TV access in Guatemala City must be substantially more that 6 percent and should bear further investigation.

Remember that cable TV reaches most of Latin America, except for the remote areas of countries with a high percentage of indigenous peoples. That means cable networks like CNN and Home Box Office are seen regularly. A wide range of cable channels have Spanish-language time slots for virtually all types of programming.

Radio is also a popular advertising media. In Jamaica, 80 percent of the population has access to radios. This would be a viable media for spot commercials. However, radio advertising in El Salvador or Paraguay, each with only 18 percent of the population having access to radios, would be wasted.

Stay away from telemarketing. No country has enough telephone lines to enable telemarketers to cost-effectively reach a reasonable number of people. (Even in the larger cities, the average Latin American is not accustomed to telemarketing and would be unlikely to make a buying decision based on a telephone call.) In Chile, for example, 21 percent of approximately 16 million people own a telephone. If you decide to use telemarketing and call every telephone owner, you will make 3,360,000 calls (16 million times 21 percent). Assuming that one-fourth of those called answer the phone, that's 840,000 people. Now assume that you successfully sell your product to 3 percent of those who answered; that's 25,200 customers. Using these numbers, your potential customer base is two-tenths of 1 percent of the population, not a very high ratio when you calculate how much it will cost to make 3,360,000 calls.

In large metropolises such as São Paulo, Rio de Janeiro, or Buenos Aires, daily newspapers are a great place to advertise consumer goods. National circulation statistics do not tell the whole story, however. Every work day, office workers and professionals in the commercial districts of these cities can be seen busily poring over the local newspaper. Suburbanites page through the dailies to learn about upcoming entertainment, social, and political events. Consumer ads are as hard to ignore in these newspapers as they are in U.S. papers.

Magazines are also a viable media, especially trade periodicals for industrial and commercial goods. Many industries have their own trade journals. Potential customers in other industries can be reached through monthly or quarterly magazines. Unfortunately, statistical tabulations of magazine readerships in Latin America are not kept current, and those that are published by trade magazines reflect only limited, not broad readership.

Latin Americans in urban areas love to attend movies. Advertisements that immediately precede a featured movie will reach captive audiences that may not be otherwise receptive. These ads can be quite expensive, however, so you might do better with other media, at least until you establish brand recognition.

Although television, radio, newspapers, or cinema ads may bring desired results in urban markets, billboards with flashy pictures and mobile hawkers with high-amplification speakers are very effective in remote areas and in less-developed countries such as Guyana. Displays in public-transit buses and vans also reach a large audience, especially in metropolitan areas.

Since many people who will see your advertisement cannot read, or can read very little, use plenty of attractive pictures and illustrations rather than words. Nearly any type of illustration conveys brand recognition and creates moods better than does the written word. Stay away from slogans, double entendres, and idioms that can easily backfire.

Internet Advertising

A lot of people believe that Internet advertising is the wave of the future. That may be so in a decade or two, but it hasn't reached such a pinnacle yet. However, a handful of Latin American countries are enjoying a rapid rise in Internet advertising. Brazil and Mexico, for instance, comprise the region's largest Internet advertising markets, together capturing 73 percent of total expenditures.

According to the *Global Entertainment and Media Outlook: 2005–2009,* published by PricewaterhouseCoopers, increased broadband access will be the principal driving force causing increased Internet access worldwide but not in Latin America.

Throughout the region, telephony infrastructure is still grossly inferior to the rest of the world, and until that changes, traditional dial-up service in those countries with sufficient landline penetration will be the main Internet access method. PricewaterhouseCoopers forecasts that Internet access in Latin America will grow at a compound annual growth rate of 22.3 percent, reaching $7.2 billion by 2009. **Table 9-2** shows the percentage of populations with access to the Internet for each country.

Table 9-2 | Internet Users As a Percent of Population

Country	Internet Users (Million)	Population (Million)	Percent of Population
Chile	6.7	16.1	43
Jamaica	1.1	2.8	39
Argentina	10.0	39.9	25
Costa Rica	1.0	4.1	24
Uruguay	0.7	3.4	21
Trinidad/Tobago	0.2	1.1	18
Mexico	17.0	107.4	16
Peru	4.6	28.3	16
Brazil	25.9	188.1	14
Guyana	0.1	0.8	13
Venezuela	3.0	25.7	12
Colombia	4.7	43.6	10
Panama	0.3	3.1	10
Dominican Republic	0.8	9.2	9
El Salvador	0.6	6.8	9
Guatemala	0.8	12.3	7
Ecuador	0.6	13.5	4

Bolivia	0.3	9.0	3
Honduras	0.2	7.3	3
Paraguay	0.1	6.5	2
Nicaragua	0.1	5.6	2
Canada	20.9	33.1	63
United States	203.8	298.4	68

Source: Internet World Stats; CIA Factbook, 2006

As Latin American economic conditions improve and the political scene stabilizes, the region will experience increased investment in telephony infrastructure. This will, in turn, drive increased Internet usage. As Internet access increases, so will Internet advertising expenditures. PricewaterhouseCoopers predicts that the Internet advertising market in Latin America will grow at a 33 percent compound annual rate and reach $337 million by 2009. Such a growth rate seems remarkable; however, the benefits of Internet advertising will only be realized when users actually buy products online. Latin America isn't ready for this yet. Antiquated banking systems and weak bank regulations have held back the use of credit cards. Still, in those few countries with an active credit-card market, online retailing is a very viable strategy. The Boston Consulting Group judged that Latin American online retail sales topped $3.8 billion in 2003. That's a lot of online buying.

Although credit-card purchases lag U.S. usage by a wide margin, debit cards are increasingly popular and the payment method of choice for most online purchases. Latin American consumers like to pay as they go rather than be saddled with exorbitant interest payments on credit cards. According to Visa International's Miami office, debit cards account for 80 percent of the company's 120 million cards in Latin American circulation.

The Boston Consulting Group's *Online Retailing in Latin America: Beyond the Storefront* states that the following are the major obstacles to be overcome in Latin American online retailing:

- Late fulfillment of orders
- Poor response to customer service requests
- Poor product selection
- Alternative payment methods rather than credit cards
- Distrust of Internet financial security

These shortcomings open the door for companies to place ads assuring customers of rapid fulfillment, excellent customer service, and wide product selection; welcoming debit card use; and promising high-level security. Incorporating these positives in your ads should bring excellent responses to all types of consumer products.

Although online credit-card purchasing has been slow to launch, it is beginning to take hold. A market research firm, InfoAmericas, reports that in 2005, more than 1 million Latin merchants accepted them. Add this increased use of credit cards to the already popular debit cards, and online retailing seems ready to take off. It looks like those analysts who predicted Internet advertising would be the wave of the future will be proven prescient.

In 2005, The Economist Intelligence Unit undertook a study of various ways for consumers to pay for purchases in six countries: Argentina, Brazil, Chile, Colombia, Mexico, and Venezuela. The study found vast improvements had occurred in electronic payment systems. All nations except Venezuela had introduced Real Time Gross Settlement (RTGS) systems. Argentina initiated a five-point discount in the country's 21 percent VAT rate for debit cards and a three-point discount for credit cards. Brazil is now able to make same-day customer-initiated direct transfers. Chile connected the country's entire ATM network and introduced smart cards for payment on the Santiago transit system. Colombia introduced a two-point VAT rebate. Mexico, which has the most advanced credit-card system in the region, is using smart cards as promotions. It also discourages the use of bank checks by stretching the bank processing time for clearing them. Venezuela has increased credit-card payment processing speed. With these countries leading the way, the rest of Latin America will surely follow in relatively short order.

Before investing a sizable piece of your advertising budget in the Internet or any other media, it would be beneficial to know how many people will actually read or listen to your ads. A Mexican market research firm, Moctezuma y Asociados, reported in their survey *TGI Mexico* that entertainment-seeking Internet users always paid attention to advertising media in the following percentages:

- Television: 20.2 percent
- Radio: 8.2 percent
- Newspaper: 9.4 percent
- Magazines: 7.9 percent
- Internet: 21.5 percent

Information-seeking Internet users always paid attention to advertisements in the following percentages:

- Television: 27.7 percent
- Radio: 15 percent
- Newspaper: 11.6 percent
- Magazines: 10.2 percent
- Internet: 19.8 percent

With about 20 percent of both groups of Internet users paying close attention to Internet ads, this is clearly a productive advertising media, at least in those countries with good access to the Internet. More than that, you get double coverage from Internet ads because when you run Spanish-language ads on the Internet, you also reach Hispanic Internet users living in the United States. This huge market is growing every year. Add this to the number of potential consumers who live in Latin America, and the market size for Internet advertising goes well beyond that of any other media.

Trade Shows

The easiest and most popular way to check out a new market and simultaneously introduce your company name and product line is by exhibiting at a Latin American trade show. This is an excellent way to get a firsthand look at local competitors. It is also a convenient arena for meeting potential distributors and sales representatives. Be aware, however, that exhibiting in Latin America may involve significantly different logistics than those found in the United States. Some of the key questions to resolve ahead of time are the following:

- What are booths called? Stands, tables, compartments, or booths?
- What type of pipe-and-drape configurations are used?
- Are booth dimensions metric? What are the maximum, minimum, and customary sizes?
- How are booths constructed? Modular components, hard walls, curtains?
- How many exhibitors will be at the show?
- What is the normal attendance?
- From how big a region does the trade show draw exhibitors and attendees?
- How do you get samples, displays, and equipment through customs if the country does not abide by the carnet convention?
- What type of facility houses the show, and where is it located relative to hotels, air terminals, and ports?

Regardless of the answers to these questions, let your local sales representative make the arrangements. Don't try to do it from the United States, or you can be sure something will go wrong.

Take as much care as you can in designing your display booth and promotion literature. If you hope to sell anything through an exposition, your booth as well as your literature must be customized to meet local tastes without compromising the identity of your company and its products. And, of course, you must sell, sell, sell. The experiences of two U.S. exporters with adjacent booths at a trade show in São Paulo provide an interesting comparison.

A machine tool salesman manned a large booth replete with three gorgeous models, a variety of sales literature, free wine, and a continuously running video. Potential customers, suppliers, and curiosity seekers were drawn to the booth like flies to flypaper, resulting in hundreds of valuable sales leads. The adjacent booth was draped with purple bunting, stocked with single-sheet copies of a sales memo, and manned part-time by one salesman wearing a wrinkled wool suit that made him look as if he had just returned from an eighteen-hour flight. His company's name was painted on a white sheet of paper hung from the back of the booth, although it was hard to tell exactly what he was selling. Over a three-day period, this ragtag salesman collected just six business cards.

If you are going to exhibit at trade shows, do it right. Get advice from experts. And, as with any type of advertising or sales promotion, those experts should be familiar with the design, message, and promotion gimmicks necessary to attract customers in that locale.

Since advertising is so important for breaking into and sustaining Latin American markets, it makes good sense to find a cost-effective way to use this tool. With a little effort and creativity, an advertising program can be designed and managed to get good results with a minimum of expense. But knowing your customers and thoroughly understanding the external forces that affect your ability to reach them are still the key ingredients to success.

Chapter 10

Trade Finance

Whether your plans call for a Latin American manufacturing or distribution presence, a joint venture, or are limited to exporting, someone will have to provide the financing. Take exporting. Unless you know your customer very well, you probably would not sell on open account. Customer credit references may or may not be current or reliable, and collecting from recalcitrant customers can be a nightmarish task. So what do you do? How do you help your customer arrange financing? Fortunately, many federal and state agencies, private organizations, and international banks offer a variety of options.

As for collections, credit insurance is the only way to go. You can get it to cover losses from customers who refuse to pay, political expropriation, breach of contract, and many other causes. While it is certainly possible to do business in Latin America without such insurance, that doesn't seem prudent when coverage against practically any contingency is readily available.

Trade finance is the key to profitable exporting. Nine times out of ten, the financing you offer determines whether you or your competitor gets the order. So as a marketing tool, trade finance provides a competitive advantage as readily as do price discounts, after-the-sale customer service, or free deliveries. Moreover, customized trade finance strategies are crucial to success regardless of the country your customer resides in. Here is a personal experience with a Caribbean customer that demonstrates the point.

A few years ago, I owned a manufacturing company that designed and produced a wide range of metal parts for the automotive after-market and for off-road construction equipment manufacturers. My marketing vice president romanced several contractors who were bidding on a massive industrial project in Trinidad and Tobago. One that he was especially interested in seemed to be in the driver's seat to win a major bid. This contractor also had strong political connections in the Trinidadian government. I cautioned this supersalesman that we must be prepared to offer long-term financing for an order whose shipments would surely extend over four or five years. He disagreed and insisted that the contractor pay cash in advance for one-half the order and open a straight letter of credit for the other half. The customer rebelled, we lost the order, and the marketing vice president lost his job.

Trade finance is a key element in your marketing plans. It is just as important to success in Latin America as product design, pricing, and customer service. Why? Because Latin customers, both government agencies and private-sector companies, expect exporters to help arrange financing for them to pay for the goods. Several countries in the region have very weak financial systems. Banks are unable or unwilling to grant import credit. Export-import banks are either non-existent or too small to finance larger import orders. Without home-grown bank support, customers in these countries must look to foreign exporters for trade finance. Moreover, European and Asian competitors stand ready to offer trade finance of various tenure, forcing U.S. exporters to do the same.

This chapter explores a variety of trade finance strategies, together with ways to guarantee the timely collection of customer accounts. Some methods are available only through U.S. government-sponsored programs, some derive from state and city agencies, and others can be arranged through private means. To help organize the vast array of options, these finance strategies can be divided into four categories, according to the payment schedule negotiated in the sales contract:

1. Short-term strategies, when payment terms are less than 180 days
2. Intermediate-term strategies, when payment terms run from six months to five years
3. Long-term strategies, when payment periods are greater than five years
4. Countertrade strategies, when customers cannot or will not pay in hard currency

Short-Term Strategies

The most common forms of short-term trade finance, documentary letters of credit and banker's acceptances, place the collection burden on banks. Occasionally, open-account terms may be used, but that is the exception rather than the rule. Unless your customer has an excellent credit rating, is willing to securitize the transaction with accessible collateral, or you know the principals very well, stay away from open-account sales.

Documentary Letters of Credit

A documentary letter of credit (L/C) can be used to reduce the risk of nonpayment or delay of payment. It is called documentary because the terms of the letter specify payment against the presentation of certain sales and shipping documents. Nearly all letters of credit used in international trade are documentary. Payment terms may involve sight or time drafts or other demands for payment. Time drafts are also referred to as *usance* drafts.

L/Cs do not, in and of themselves, guarantee payment and should not be substituted for common-sense credit judgment. The instructions embodied in the L/C determine the payment security. Therefore, specific instructions must be written into the L/C in such a manner that payment will be made in compliance with the sales contract.

Letters of credit come in many forms and carry a wide range of provisions. They can be revocable or irrevocable, confirmed or advised, straight or negotiated, payable at sight or over an extended period of time, transferable, assignable, or restricted. They can be written to cover partial shipments, full shipments, or transshipments. An L/C can cover one shipment, or it may be revolving, covering several subsequent shipments.

Regardless of other provisions, L/Cs should be irrevocable and confirmed by an American bank. (When I refer to American banks, I include the U.S. operating branches of foreign-owned banks.) *Irrevocable* means that the issuer cannot change the terms of the L/C, and *confirmed* means that an American bank is obligated to make payment upon presentation of proper documentation. Proper documentation means bills of lading or other transport documents, proving that the goods have in fact been delivered as specified in the order. However, L/Cs must be properly prepared and executed to be valid. A bank will not honor an L/C unless all supporting documentation called for in the letter accompanies a payment request. Here is an example of what happens when payment is made against an irrevocable letter of credit confirmed by a U.S. bank:

1. After the exporter (call it Miami Sales, Inc.) and its customer (call it Rio Markets, Ltd.) agree on the terms of a sale, Rio Markets arranges for its bank, say Chase Manhattan, to open a letter of credit.
2. Chase prepares an irrevocable L/C in favor of Miami Sales, including all negotiated instructions covering the shipment.
3. Chase sends the L/C to a U.S. bank, say Citibank, requesting confirmation.
4. Citibank prepares a letter of confirmation and sends it to Miami Sales, along with the L/C.
5. Miami Sales carefully reviews all conditions in the L/C to be certain that the conditions agree with the negotiated terms. Miami Sales's freight forwarder is then contacted

to make sure the shipping date can be met. (If Miami Sales cannot comply with one or more of the conditions, Rio Markets is immediately contacted to arrange new language for the L/C.)

6. Miami Sales arranges with its freight forwarder to deliver the goods to the appropriate port or air terminal.
7. When the goods are loaded, the forwarder completes the necessary documents, including the bill of lading.
8. Miami Sales, or its freight forwarder, presents the documentation to Citibank.

Citibank reviews the documents and if they are in order sends them to Chase for review and transmittal to Rio Markets. Rio Markets, or its agent, then uses the documents to claim the goods upon their arrival in Brazil. On the date specified in the L/C, Citibank honors the draft that accompanies the letter of credit. As an alternative, Citibank may discount the draft for payment at an earlier date.

No matter how carefully we prepare L/Cs, errors that prevent payment seem to creep in. Here are the most common ones:

- Omission of clauses stating "irrevocable" or "confirmed by [a designated American bank]"
- Misspelled name and/or address of exporter or customer
- Credit insufficient to cover full cost of shipment, including forwarding fees, consular fees, insurance, inspection charges, etc.
- Incomplete or inaccurate description of merchandise, prices, and terms of payment
- Failure to allow for variations in shipping quantity due to shrinkage, damaged goods, etc.
- Omission of the words "about" or "approximately" (which allow for 10 percent variance) preceding the amount of credit

- Marks and numbers on invoice different from those on other documents
- Wording in customer's draft different from that in the L/C
- Inappropriate or incomplete markings on bill of lading that do not conform to L/C instructions
- Bill of lading shipping date later than allowed in L/C
- Failure of all drafts and other documents to carry a date prior to the expiration date of the L/C
- Instructions in L/C different from those specified in the invoice

Variations on Documentary Letters of Credit

There are many variations on a straightforward documentary letter of credit, far too many to be included here. Here are the most common options:

- Back-to-back L/Cs are used when vendors or subcontractors demand payment from the exporter before collections are received from the customer.
- Off-balance-sheet credit extension is a variation on the back-to-back L/C theme. By extending off-balance-sheet credit, a bank uses the exporter's general credit line, not the buyer's L/C as collateral, permitting the bank to issue new L/Cs direct to the exporter's vendors.
- Assigned proceeds can be used when an exporter desires to use a buyer's credit to raise working capital. This is achieved by assigning the proceeds from the buyer's L/C to companies that supply the exporter with parts and materials.
- Transferred L/Cs are used when exporters require that certain materials or products be shipped direct from their supplier to the foreign customer rather than relayed to the exporter's for inclusion in the complete order. Terms of payment, shipping instructions,

insurance provisions, product markings, drawdown documentation, and all other terms and conditions stipulated in the letter of credit remain intact.

• Standby letters of credit are used as guarantees of performance or payment in lieu of bank guarantees. They are essentially unsecured lines of credit to customers.

When your customer does not have sufficient credit or capital to warrant the issuance of a confirmed, irrevocable L/C as immediate payment, other financing instruments can be used. A documentary banker's acceptance is one such possibility.

Documentary Banker's Acceptances

A documentary banker's acceptance (BA) is an instrument that guarantees payment to an exporter directly from a customer's bank. This eliminates any risk of non-payment, thereby eliminating any credit risk for the exporter. Here is how BAs work:

1. Quito Electronics wants to buy a shipment of TVs, radios, and computers from U.S. Electronics but can't afford to pay in advance. Also, Quito Electronics has not yet established its credit with U.S. Electronics.

2. Quito Electronics asks its Ecuadorian bank to issue a draft to U.S. Electronics for the full amount of the shipment, based on Quito Electronics' credit record with that bank. The draft's payment date is set at two weeks after the shipment arrives in Quito, Ecuador.

3. Since the Ecuadorian bank knows that its customer is good for the amount of the draft, the bank "accepts" the draft on behalf of Quito Electronics. The bank stamps the draft with its acceptance stamp and sends it on to U.S. Electronics.

4. U.S. Electronics takes the accepted draft to its U.S. bank and receives payment for the shipment. The U.S. bank

then collects the amount from the Ecuadorian bank. In two weeks, Quito Electronics settles the draft with its Ecuadorian bank.

Both sides win with banker's acceptances. As an exporter, you get your cash immediately, while your customer conserves cash for the holding period.

One glitch may arise to invalidate the BA, leaving your bank and therefore your company holding worthless paper. That can happen when your Latin customer and a Latin bank collude to defraud. Either the Latin bank doesn't exist, is in financial default, or doesn't have sufficient capital to match the draft. Each of these circumstances has actually happened. Therefore it is crucial to determine that your customer's bank is in fact good for the BA before you agree to ship products. Your U.S. bank should be able to verify this, or you can contact the International Chamber of Commerce for confirmation. Its address is International Chamber of Commerce, 38 cours Albert 1er, 75008 Paris, France.

Getting Paid

After arranging financing for customers, it's only prudent to ensure that you get paid. Since you have virtually no legal recourse in the United States if your Latin American customer breaches a sales contract, other collection methods must be in place.

Before making the first shipment, be sure to verify your customer's credit rating. Fortunately, several organizations, both federal and private, offer credit reports on foreign customers. Be aware, however, that Latin American credit reports tend to be outdated and inaccurate.

This is where the U.S. Commercial Service (USCS) can be very helpful. The USCS is the promotion arm of the International Trade Administration. One of its missions is to help small and mid-size U.S. exporters. In addition to other assistance, it will provide you "with an opinion as to the viability and reliability of the overseas company or individual you have selected as well as an opinion on the relative strength of that company's industry sector in your target market."

It does this by issuing International Company Profile (ICP) background reports. These reports include the following:

- Detailed credit standing on prospective Latin American target customers, potential sales representatives, or prospective partners
- A listing of that company's key officers and senior management
- Banking and other financial information about the company
- Market information, including a company's public-record sales and profit history

Dun & Bradstreet and a few smaller credit bureaus provide reports on larger companies, but they are not necessarily reliable or current. Commercial banks are a better source of credit reports. All major banks maintain their own credit departments, and chances are good that your bank can get credit information on virtually any customer who has purchased goods from an American company within the past few years.

You can also get a credit report online from a British company: International Company Profiles, 6-14 Underwood Street, London N1 7JQ.

Eximbank's Credit Insurance

In addition to checking credit reports, it makes sense to purchase credit insurance. Insurance against both political and commercial risk is available from private carriers or from Eximbank. Eximbank issues five types of policies that cover a wide range of risks, including expropriation, customer's failure to pay, and currency fluctuations:

- New-to-export policies for short-term credit sales of companies just getting started in exporting
- Umbrella policies that are available only to export agents such as EMCs, and ETCs that administer single policies on behalf of multiple exporters
- Multibuyer policies for companies that export to several buyers in the same country
- Short- and medium-term single-buyer policies that cover several exporting companies shipping to a single buyer, such as a government agency or a state-owned electric company
- Operating lease policies that cover lease payments and the value of leased products

Private Insurance Companies

Of the few private insurance companies that sell export policies, AIG Political Risks, Inc., a subsidiary of American International Group, Inc., is probably the most active. It insures against expropriation, money transfer loss, and contract repudiation by foreign governments. It also sells performance bonds required in bidding arrangements.

FCIA Management Company, a wholly owned subsidiary of Great American Insurance Company of Cincinnati, part of American Financial Group, is another comprehensive insurer of all types of potential export losses. At one time FCIA was a subsidiary of Eximbank, but in the early 1990s it was spun off to the private sector. Between FCIA and AIG Political Risks, you should be able to get all the export coverage you'll ever need.

Intermediate-Term Strategies

When a sales order calls for payments that extend over periods of from 180 days to ten years, intermediate-term financing is necessary. Although the Private Export Funding Corporation and Eximbank provide intermediate-term financing, their strong suit is funding long-term orders. Intermediate-term orders can be financed more effectively with forfaiting, factoring, leasing, or alternative transaction financing.

Forfaiting

How would you like to do this:

- Negotiate a sales contract with payment terms well beyond one year, and perhaps as much as ten years, without risk or the attendant problems of collecting against a dated letter of credit?
- Get paid 100 percent of the selling price when the shipment is made?
- Have your customer pay all financing costs?

If that sounds appealing, you may want to look into forfaiting, a relatively new technique in the United States, although one used for many years by European exporters.

The middleman in a forfaiting transaction is a forfaiter, which is a specialized type of bank or lending institution that deals in the nonrecourse financing of export sales. Several non-bank organizations offer forfaiting services, as do a half-dozen or so U.S. money center banks and virtually all European and Canadian banks. None of these institutions, however, forfaits short-term orders. The forfaiting process is best suited to customers who need medium-term credit of from three to eight years but cannot obtain buyer credit from other sources.

Forfaiting is also popular under the following circumstances:

- Direct buyer credit is too complex to arrange.
- Export credit insurance is not available.
- Competitors offer forfaiting.
- Buyers insist on fixed-rate financing to close the order.

Export orders can be as large as $50 million or as small as $50,000. The forfaiting procedure is relatively simple. This is how it works:

1. A customer seeking intermediate-term credit negotiates with an exporter a series of notes, drafts, bills, or other instruments. These documents will be used to pay off balances due the exporter over the term of the transaction.
2. The exporter then contacts a forfaiter, and the forfaiter and the customer negotiate with a bank, usually the customer's bank, to guarantee the customer's note, draft, or bill. The simplicity of this transaction has great appeal to both bankers and customers because no contracts are involved that could require litigation in the event of default.
3. Finally, when the exporter presents the forfaiter with a complete set of documentation, the forfaiter releases the funds.

Forfaiting has four broad advantages:

1. It provides medium- to long-term financing when short-term credit won't work.
2. It covers the entire sale, not just 85 percent of the contract value, which is the maximum covered by Eximbank.
3. It costs less than borrowing from a commercial bank.
4. In its simplest form, forfaiting is very much like traditional accounts-receivable factoring, except that forfaiting requires a bank guarantee from the customer. Forfaiting isn't for everyone. But if it does fit your needs, it is one of the fastest and cheapest ways to finance a medium-term export order.

Forfaiting transactions are mostly handled by European financial institutions. However, a few have sprung up in the United States. Trade and Export Finance Online is a California company that can help you find one when you are ready. Its Web site (see Appendix F) also carries a very good description of the pluses and minuses of forfaiting. Standard

Bank of South Africa has a forfait department and a New York branch office. The London Forfaiting Company in New York has been active in forfaiting for many years. It was recently taken over by the First International Merchant Bank of Malta, which has expanded its U.S. forfaiting activities. British American Forfaiting Company of St. Louis is one of the more active U.S. forfaiting houses and can be reached at #1 The Pines Court, St. Louis, MO 63141. This company will forfait transactions over $100,000, and you can get a quote by completing a form on the company's Web site (included in Appendix F). If all else fails, you can get names and contact information of forfaiters from the trade association: International Forfaiting Association, P.O. Box 432, CH-8024 Zurich, Switzerland.

Export Factoring

Most people are familiar with factoring domestic receivables and the stigma of financial difficulties that attaches to it. Export factoring brings far greater benefits without the stigma. Export factoring does, however, involve selling receivables at a discount, usually 70 to 90 percent of the invoice value. But once that is done, your company is off the hook for any collection default. In other words, the factor assumes commercial risk and political risk. Export factors provide a variety of other services as well, including credit investigations, bookkeeping functions, monthly reports issued to the exporter, and a choice of payment cycles.

If export factoring seems like a viable option, your best bet is to contact one of the following international factoring organizations through their Web sites, listed in Appendix F, to get the names and addresses of reputable export factors in your area:

- Factors Chain International is a global network of leading factoring companies, whose common aim is to facilitate international trade through factoring and related financial services. This network claims to represent 206 factors in fifty-nine countries. These factors presumably handle more than 50 percent of the world's cross-border export factoring.

- International Factors is an international factoring association with seventy-eight members in fifty countries.
- First Commercial Credit is a large factor house that also does other types of trade finance.

Alternative Transaction Financing

The reluctance of commercial banks to look beyond a company's balance sheet to determine its creditworthiness has opened the door to a variety of nonbank organizations that specialize in trade finance. These organizations finance individual export transactions rather than entire companies. In other words, their level of interest is determined by the viability of a specific export order, not by a company's profitability or debt-to-equity ratio.

Some of these transaction-finance organizations are outgrowths of state foreign-trade programs. Others are privately owned by manufacturing, shipping, distribution, or trading companies. Still others are subsidiaries of major international commercial and investment banks.

Transaction finance is ideally suited to companies that are entering new Latin American markets, partnering with new Latin suppliers or customers, or investing in new inventory for seasonal reasons or to re-stock a single customer. Transaction finance also applies to companies who need to finance large, single-export orders while leaving current borrowing facilities intact. And it works well in tandem with export factoring, especially when factor houses cannot handle staggered payments.

Most private-sector transaction finance organizations specialize in a particular form of trade credit or in specific industries. They offer a variety of finance services, including factoring, forfaiting, foreign-exchange management, loans, and equity contributions (primarily for companies interested in establishing maquila plants). Check out Creative Capital Associates based outside Washington, D.C., or InternetLC. com based in California. (See Appendix F for contact information.) Alternately, get the names of transaction finance organizations in your area from your state export trade promotion bureau or a money center bank.

Small Business Administration (SBA)

Export financing assistance from the SBA Office of International Trade encompasses three programs: SBA Export*Express*, the Export Working Capital Program, and the International Trade Loan Program. To contact this SBA office, use the Web site listed in Appendix F.

Bank loans through the SBA Export*Express* guarantee program can be used for several purposes:

- Financing export-development activities such as participating in a foreign trade show or translation of product literature
- Revolving lines of credit for export purposes
- Standby letters of credit used as bid or performance bonds on foreign contracts
- Transaction-specific financing associated with the completion of actual export orders
- Acquiring, constructing, renovating, improving, or expanding facilities and equipment to be used in the United States for the production of goods or services for export

For qualified exporters, the SBA will guarantee 85 percent of bank loans of up to $150,000 and 75 percent of loans between $150,000 and $250,000. Exporters must negotiate loan terms with their own banks but within the restrictions imposed by the SBA. Lenders may charge up to 6.5 percent over prime rate for loans of $50,000 or less and 4.5 percent over prime for loans over $50,000. Maturities generally run five to ten years for working capital loans and ten to fifteen years for equipment loans.

Export Working Capital Loan Program

The SBA's Export Working Capital Loan (EWCL) program is a handy way to finance export sales when you have already reached your borrowing limit with your bank. Under this program, the SBA guarantees up to 90 percent of the loan amount up to $1 million for exports comprising either a single transaction or multiple transactions on a revolving basis. When an EWCL is combined with an SBA International Trade Loan, the guarantee can go up to $1.25 million. EWCL financing may be used for the following purposes:

- Purchase of finished goods or other inventory for export
- Pre-export costs of labor and materials used in the manufacture of goods to be exported
- Cost of U.S. labor and overhead for service-company exports
- Standby letters of credit used for bid or performance bonds
- Foreign accounts receivable for exports sold on open account

The SBA charges a guaranty fee of one-quarter of 1 percent on the guaranteed portion of the loan for maturities of twelve months or less. It insists on the following loan collateral:

- A first lien on all items financed by the EWCL, including export inventory and foreign receivables
- The assignment of proceeds from letters of credit, documentary collections, and foreign accounts receivables
- Personal guarantees of key principals or owners of 20 percent or more of the exporting company

International Trade Loan Program

SBA guarantees under the International Trade Loan (ITL) program can go as high as $1.25 million in combined working capital loans and facilities and equipment loans. Either the working capital portion or the fixed asset portion can be up to $1 million, but the two together cannot exceed $1.25 million. Maturities of up to ten years apply to working capital loans and maturities up to twenty-five years apply to fixed asset loans.

Proceeds under the ITL can be used for the purchase or renovation of buildings and equipment located in the United States and used to produce export goods. The working capital portion can be transaction-specific or permanent. Coverage is 85 percent on loans up to $150,000 and 75 percent on loans above $150,000, up to $1.25 million.

Long-Term Strategies

There are three federal-government–related sources of long-term trade finance: the Private Export Funding Corporation, Eximbank, and U.S. Department of Agriculture programs. In addition, several states and cities have started export finance and development agencies that operate in conjunction with Eximbank's City-State Partners Initiative.

Private Export Funding Corporation

The Private Export Funding Corporation (PEFCO) is owned by several U.S. banks and large corporations and is closely associated with Eximbank. PEFCO's mission is to bridge the gap between Eximbank's long-term financing and short-term bank instruments. Loans go directly to foreign buyers of U.S. exports or to intermediary financial institutions for on-lending to foreign buyers. Although financing packages with unique interest rate and repayment terms can be structured on a case-by-case basis, nearly all require Eximbank guarantees.

PEFCO is considered a supplemental lender. As such, it enters a transaction only when financing is not available from traditional sources. Its principal contribution to the world of exporting has been that it can make long-term loans with fixed interest rates during periods of tight credit. PEFCO loans range from $1 million to well over $100 million. Applications should be made through your commercial bank.

Eximbank

Although the trade finance options discussed so far may be all you need to close an order, in the end, you might have to consider Eximbank. Eximbank goes beyond what banks can do and offers both medium- and long-term trade finance. Officially, any U.S. exporter of any size and in any industry can use Eximbank services. In practice, however, Eximbank is more responsive to larger manufacturing companies. I have known a few smaller exporters who have used Eximbank, but usually this government agency requires far too much collateral from small businesses.

The following main programs are offered by Eximbank:

- Pre-Export Guarantees are for working capital loans used to produce export orders.
- Buyer Financing covers 75 percent of the contract price after a 15 percent cash down payment by the buyer.
- Structured and Project Financing is for the construction and operation of infrastructure and other projects.
- Transportation Equipment Financing is for exports of airplanes, locomotives, rolling stock, ships, and trucks.

Although Eximbank offers direct loans and loan guarantees throughout the Western Hemisphere, it is especially active in Brazil. Political developments in Bolivia and Venezuela have reduced the bank's interest in these countries.

Countertrade Strategies

Exporters always prefer hard currency. However, to compete against European and Asian rivals, it is sometimes necessary to negotiate countertrade arrangements specifically suited to a given customer.

What is countertrade? Countertrade is a contractual arrangement that links exports from one country and imports to another country with the limited use, or no use, of currency. Although many people have tried to define countertrade more succinctly, it defies pigeonholing. Barter, offsets, parallel trade, and buybacks are terms used to describe various forms of the same concept, namely, that of giving up something of value (exported products) in exchange for something else of value (cash, products, or services).

For many years, countertrade was the exclusive domain of military hardware suppliers. Lockheed, Boeing, Grumman, General Dynamics, and so on used countertrade to sell airplanes, guns, and ships to foreign buyers. Selling into currency-poor countries in Africa encouraged global pharmaceutical companies to use countertrade in place of currency. Today, the biggest countertraders are Lockheed Martin, Boeing Ventures, British Aerospace, the European ABB Structured Finance division of ABB, and Siemens KFU. For many years global estimates attributed 40 to 50 percent of all world trade to some form of countertrade. In 2003, FDI Magazine quoted the United Kingdom's minister for international trade, Baroness Symons, as claiming that this ratio was closer to 10 to 15 percent of world trade. Interviews that I have had with several marketing and financial executives of U.S. and Latin American-based companies indicate that countertrade accounts for more than half of all trade between Latin America and the United States. Whichever ratio is correct, it seems clear that in Latin America, and especially in South America, the use of countertrade as a primary marketing tool rather than a financing technique is becoming more popular every year.

Those companies that have engaged in countertrade seem to agree that it is not as efficient as the free-market, multilateral system. It is complex, risky, and sometimes costly.

Clearly, many exporters, especially smaller companies, will not be able to use countertrade effectively. Nevertheless, those that can use it will find countertrade to be a rational and practical approach to difficult international economic circumstances, such as a lack of foreign exchange, protectionism, structural limitations, and other external market risks found throughout Latin America.

Countertrade contracts vary with each deal and from customer to customer. Their form and content are limited only by the imagination of the parties involved. Some contracts involve only the exporter and its customer. Others involve third or even fourth parties. Countertrade contracts may entail payment entirely in goods or services, or payment partly in goods and services and partly in cash. The cash portion may be denominated in the currency of the buyer or in that of the exporter. Moreover, a contract may require additional services to be performed either by the exporter or by the buyer beyond the mere delivery of goods. The many variations of countertrade can be discussed under several broad headings:

- Barter
- Compensation
- Parallel trade
- Counterpurchase
- Offsets
- Buybacks
- Co-production

Barter is the oldest form of countertrade and involves exchanging one type of product or service for another. The amount exchanged from each party is determined by negotiation, without invoicing or any exchange of money. To make a barter arrangement work, both parties must either be able to use the goods or sell them at a profit.

Compensation is merely a variation on the barter theme. In this case, the exporter is paid a combination of goods and currency, with the currency denominated either in U.S. dollars or in the buyer's home currency. In the latter case, of course, the exporter must either convert the soft currency to a hard currency or use it in the buyer's country. As with straightforward barter, the exporter must either use the exchanged goods internally or sell them, usually through a countertrade broker.

Parallel trade involves two separate contracts, one for the export sale and one for the purchase of goods from the buyer. Export insurance underwriters as well as trade finance institutions require two contracts so that each side of the transaction may be enforced individually.

Counterpurchase is one of the terms used to describe a parallel trade arrangement involving actual cash transfers. Under such an arrangement, exporter and customer each pay the other for the goods received with drafts, letters of credit, or wire transfers. These payments may both be in one currency, or they may be denominated in the home currency of each party. Many knowledgeable Latin American governments encourage counterpurchase arrangements as a way to balance imports and exports as well as to stabilize their currencies and control inflationary pressures.

Offsets are a more complex form of parallel trade. They may involve a third, or even a fourth, party to the transaction. Exchanged goods then come from a supplier other than the exporter's customer and often from a different country altogether. Most offset transactions involve a corporate seller and a sovereign purchaser. Products are typically large, high-value items, such as aircraft, military hardware, or infrastructure equipment such as turbines, boilers, smelting furnaces, and so on. However, they may be large orders of high-value goods, such as pharmaceuticals. The deal normally involves a package of transactions carried out over a defined period of time and theoretically compensates the importing country for loss of jobs, currency exchange, and the development of similar technologies within the buyer's country. Here is how an offset transaction might be structured:

1. Assume you want to sell mining equipment to the Peruvian government, which doesn't have enough hard currency to pay for it.
2. Your company agrees to finance the building of a state-owned fertilizer plant in Peru in exchange for a 40 percent equity interest.
3. Fertilizer is then exported to Argentina for pesos, which are used by the Peruvian government to pay you for the mining equipment.
4. Your company uses the pesos to pay operating expenses in your Argentine plant. This plant produces components for your mining equipment, which is assembled in the United States.

Everyone wins in this kind of deal. The Peruvian government creates jobs, foreign exchange, and a viable industry. Most of the funding for the building of the fertilizer plant comes through the U.S. Agency for International Development. As the fertilizer business grows, you should be able to reap profits from your 40 percent equity ownership. And, of course, you succeed in closing the original export order.

Buyback arrangements are quite common for the sale of technology, licenses, production lines, or even complete factories. Many U.S. companies use buybacks to import subassemblies, components, or parts needed for the completion of finished products. Buyback products could also be sold on the open market, of course.

Buybacks are especially popular for turnkey projects such as factories, warehouses, resorts, hospitals, or infrastructure facilities. Here is an example of how a turnkey buyback transaction might be structured:

1. The customer first pays for the project with government-backed long-term credit.
2. The exporter then agrees either to buy back products or services from the completed facility or to serve as a distributor for products exported from the host country.

3. The host-country buyer uses these hard currency payments to liquidate the original long-term credit.

In a variation on this arrangement, no cash changes hands, and no credit arrangements are necessary. The countertrade contract merely states that the output from the newly constructed facility will be applied to the original price of the exports. However, with this type of arrangement, you should insist on a bank guarantee to ensure that the contracted output from the new facility will be produced and shipped on schedule.

Co-production is a specialized form of buyback countertrade used principally for the transfer of technology or management expertise. The following example describes a typical co-production arrangement:

1. Assume that you want to sell desktop printers in Chile.
2. A Chilean company wants to purchase the printers but also wants the technology to produce them at home.
3. Your two companies form a joint venture to build a suburban Santiago plant to manufacture the printers.
4. Your company takes an equity interest in the project and may also furnish management support to run the facility. In either case, the facility is usually co-constructed by exporter and customer.

Since both parties remain responsible for the operation of the facility, manufacturing the printers is known as co-production. The benefits of such as arrangement are as follows:

- With equity interests, both parties profit from printer sales.
- The Chilean customer gains new technology.
- Most important, you have made an export sale.

The terms used in countertrade—compensation, coun-terpurchase, co-production, and so on—are not essential to the structuring of a countertrade deal. You can call the deal anything you want and structure it any way you want, as long as it benefits both you and your customer.

Every countertrade deal stands alone, with features unique to that transaction. There is no set formula you can apply. There are no regulations you must follow. And, with a few minor exceptions, Latin American governments will not interfere with the details of the transaction as long as you don't violate the economic and political policies of the host country. For more information on how countertrade might fit into your marketing plans, contact the U.S. trade asso-ciation, Global Offset and Countertrade Association, 818 Connecticut Avenue NW, 12th Floor, Washington, D.C. 20006.

Chapter 11

Infrastructure Development and Project Finance

Throughout this book, a variety of external forces that shape market strategies have been examined. Government interference, fiscal improprieties, high inflation, corrupt courts, street-gang violence, collapsing banking systems, and many other conditions influence how, when, and where we focus our marketing and financial resources. One final external force must be considered: infrastructure deficiencies. By infrastructure deficiencies I mean the current dilapidated state of roadways, seaports, and airports; inadequate electricity distribution and telecom service; shortages of potable water supplies; and polluting waste-disposal facilities.

According to the World Bank's Investment Climate Surveys, 55 percent of Latin American respondents considered infrastructure deficiencies to be a major obstacle to the operation and growth of their businesses. That is the highest level of concern about this subject from any region in the world.

It isn't as if Latin nations haven't made progress over the last two decades. They definitely have. In fact, several countries have come a long way in the building of new telephone lines and electricity lines. But vast differences exist within the region. Uruguay, for instance, has sixteen times more telephone lines per capita than Haiti has. In Costa Rica, an astonishing 98 percent of households have access to electricity, a huge improvement from the 1980s; however, Peru reports that only two-thirds of its citizens have electricity.

The region has also improved the sources, storage, and distribution of safe drinking water and modernized its sewer systems (but not waste disposal facilities.) However, once again, huge differences exist, this time between rural and urban areas. The World Bank reports that 90 percent of urban households in most countries have access to safe water. But in the rural areas of Brazil and Chile, only 58 percent and 59 percent, respectively, are connected to potable water.

Access to safe drinking water is also determined by the distribution of wealth. In rural Paraguay, for instance, only 3 percent of the poorest one-fifth of the population have running potable water in their homes, while 32 percent of the richest one-fifth are connected to a potable water supply. In El Salvador, 35 percent of the poorest one-fifth have access to safe water, while 87 percent of the richest one-fifth do.

Sewer lines have been laid in most of the accessible rural areas, but sewage treatment plants are still a rarity.

No Latin country has done much to improve roadbeds, except for privatized toll roads, bridges, and tunnels. In Brazil, Peru, Nicaragua, and Mexico, less than a quarter of national highways are deemed to be in good condition. Eighty percent of roadways in Argentina meet national standards, but 20 percent do not. In urban areas of Buenos Aires, Mexico City, São Paulo, and Santiago, city streets have been maintained fairly well, but roads that surround these metropolitan areas are cracked and potholed.

On the plus side, electricity generation and distribution capability has increased in several countries. Many seaport concessions have made significant progress in upgrading their port facilities. Chile, Jamaica, Argentina, and Costa Rica have seen an explosion in Internet usage.

The World Bank conducted Enterprise Surveys for eight Latin American countries. These surveys were meant to measure infrastructure deficiencies at the household level and attempted to quantify the effect such deficiencies had on ordinary lives. **Table 11-1** shows the result of these surveys, which took place during 2003 and 2004.

Table 11-1 | Infrastructure Deficiency Indicators

Country	(1)	(2)	(3)	(4)
Brazil	20.6	3.5	0.7	12.6
Chile	6.9	2.9	0.1	7.2
Ecuador	29.5	9.5	4.1	92.7
El Salvador	12.4	7.9	16.0	6.2
Guatemala	56.1	9.5	7.3	34.3
Honduras	28.2	22.5	5.7	170.1
Nicaragua	13.4	23.0	53.1	127.6
Peru	18.6	6.1	6.8	8.1
OECD Countries	8.3	1.1	0.2	7.9

Key: (1) Days to Get Electricity Connected; (2) Days of Electricity Outage Per Year; (3) Days to Get Telephone Connected; (4) Days of Water Supply Failures
Source: World Bank Enterprise Survey, 2003 and 2004 [ETB]

Although this survey covers only eight Latin American countries, those eight countries run the gamut from most developed (Chile) to least developed (Nicaragua). Chile doesn't look too bad, with only about three days per year lost due to electrical outages. My home in Pennsylvania suffers more outages than that. Also, at 7.2 days per year, Chile has practically no water failures. At the other end of the spectrum, Nicaraguan households suffer, on average, twenty-three days per year without electricity and more than 4 months per year without water.

Overall, infrastructure development in Latin America has slipped badly in the last fifteen years. The region as a whole spends a measly 2 percent of GDP on infrastructure, while South Korea and Southeast Asia countries average almost 6 percent. One reason for Latin America's poor showing is a region-wide disenchantment with the privatizations that occurred in the 1990s. In 1990, 97 percent of telephone and electricity connections were supplied by the public sector. By 2003, 86 percent of telecoms, 60 percent of electric utilities, and 11 percent of water utilities were managed by the private sector.

Unfortunately, expectations overshadowed reality. Private-sector ownership of electric generating plants and water companies did not create enough improvements to gain acceptance by the general public. Skepticism increased. One opinion poll by BBC News found that in 2004, only one in four Latin Americans believe that privatization had been beneficial to their country, compared with 56 percent in 1998 who believed it was beneficial. Additional privatizations withered on the vine. Foreign direct investment (FDI) dropped from $109 billion in 1999 to $67 billion in 2004. Private-sector investment in infrastructures dropped from $71 billion or 86 percent of the total foreign investment in 1998 to $18.8 billion, or 28 percent of total foreign investment in 2004.

Meanwhile, governments throughout the region abdicated responsibility for infrastructure improvements. From 1996 to 2001, on average, Latin governments invested a measly 0.8 percent of their GDPs in infrastructures. The private sector nearly doubled this amount, investing 1.4 percent of GDPs, on average. This was not enough, however, to cover annual maintenance costs of about 3 percent of regional GDP, much less to build new, improved facilities. What was behind these seemingly irrational actions by Latin governments and investing companies?

Emerging from the Lost Decade of the 1980s, governments throughout Latin America were hungry for new ways to raise capital. They still had enormous external debts to repay and needed to find some way to meet these obligations other than through normal increases in GDP. Like any sensible businessperson whose company needs capital but is fully loaded with debt, these governments concluded that the solution was to sell off state assets. At that time, Latin governments owned electric utilities, telephone companies, waste treatment plants, water facilities, seaports, airports, toll roads, and many operating companies, a plethora of assets that could be turned into cash. Thus began the wave of privatizations that lasted for ten years. Caught in the euphoria of democracy in action and the beginning of market economies, citizens of every Latin country cheered their government's actions, positive that privately owned utilities would bring them a better life. Expectations soared as one foreign company after another gobbled up infrastructure facilities. However, forecasts of a glorious, rosy future turned to dust as soon as these companies found out how dilapidated the facilities that they so eagerly purchased really were. In the end, improvements came, but slowly, year by year, hardly noticeable by the general public. Latinos who had opened their arms to privatizations now turned against them, blaming the free market and private ownership for many of their country's ills.

A second feature of the privatization wave occurred simultaneously. Released from running unmanageable public utilities, governments sat back and collected their privatization capital, only too content to let private companies manage and finance infrastructure improvements. Government after government cut back infrastructure funding, shifting almost the entire financing burden on the private sector. What had been a major drain on government resources now demanded only a trickle of support.

Government abdication of the responsibility for infrastructure funding had a devastating effect on future improvements in the energy, telecom, transport, water, and sanitation sectors. With foreign companies pulling back on new investments, and in some cases disposing of their newly acquired utilities, and governments walking away from funding responsibility, infrastructure improvements almost came to a standstill, causing Latin American countries to slip further and further behind their Asian rivals.

Governments offloaded responsibility for infrastructures to the private sector at the same time that companies became increasingly alarmed by the region's political unrest, social inequities, and in the case of Argentina, Ecuador, and a few other countries, fiscal mismanagement. Companies from America, Europe, and Asia saw a region that desperately needed their help turn its back on private ownership. The World Bank's survey, *Infrastructure in Latin America and the Caribbean: Recent Developments and Key Challenges*, reported the following:

- Total investment in infrastructure in the region dropped from 37 percent of GDP in 1980–1985 to 2.2 percent of GDP in 1996–2001.
- Public-sector investment dropped from 3.1 percent of GDP to 0.8 percent of GDP for the same two periods.
- Public-sector infrastructure expenditures approximated 5 percent of total public-sector expenditures.

This report reached four conclusions:

1. The region is not spending enough on infrastructure. At about 2 percent of GDP, Latin American countries are slipping further behind South Korea and China, each of which invests 4 to 6 percent of its GDP in infrastructure.
2. The region needs to do a better job of allocating its resources. New investment must focus on improving productivity and competitiveness but not at the expense of social goals. For instance, total access to electricity, potable water, and sanitary waste disposal could be achieved over ten years by spending less than a quarter percentage point of GDP per year.
3. Governments must not abdicate responsibility for supervising and paying a fair share of infrastructure improvement. The private sector cannot and should not do it alone.
4. Governments need to establish new credibility with the private sector to encourage FDI at least equal to what it was in the early 1990s. This means reducing regulatory

risks and allowing companies to set prices that will yield an acceptable return on investment. Greater transparency in the bidding process and less corruption at the supervisory level are also needed.

The sorry state of Latin American infrastructures is not necessarily bad for business. The serious need to upgrade electricity generation and distribution, for plants to purify drinking water, and for facilities to safely dispose of waste, not to mention modern-day roads, airports, and seaports, has a silver lining for American companies. Massive projects will have to be initiated across the region, but especially in the poorer countries. Since all materials, parts, and technical and management know-how will have to be imported, American companies that have the talent, the courage, and the financial resources to participate will find a huge opportunity awaiting them. U.S. imports, from electric wire to clamps, switches, and transformers; from pumps to valves and fasteners; from heavy equipment and trucks to replacement parts for both; and a plethora of other industrial products, will fill a desperate need.

According to the UN's Conference on Trade and Development (UNCTAD) *World Investment Report, 2005,* Latin America received about $67 billion of FDI in 2004 after four consecutive years of decline. Most of it went to Brazil (27 percent) and Mexico (25 percent). But, according to the World Bank Group's *Private Participation in Infrastructure Database,* only $18.8 billion, or 28 percent of the total, was spent on infrastructure improvements. The difference, nearly $49 billion, went to building schools, apartments, office buildings, and hospitals, and to the purchase of operating businesses. **Table 11-2** shows the total FDI flows to the region for that year.

Table 11-2 Foreign Direct Investment to Latin America—2004

Country	Amount ($US Billions)
Brazil	18.2
Mexico	16.6
Chile	7.2
Argentina	4.2
Colombia	3.1
Peru	1.8
Venezuela	1.5
Ecuador	1.1
Panama	1.0
Trinidad and Tobago	1.0
Jamaica	0.7
Dominican Republic	0.6
Costa Rica	0.6
El Salvador	0.5
Uruguay	0.3
Honduras	0.3
Nicaragua	0.2
Guatemala	0.2
Paraguay	N/A
Guyana	N/A
Bolivia	N/A
Rest of Latin America	8.6

Source: UNCTAD: World Investment Report, 2005

Without question, infrastructure deficiencies severely impede productivity and competitiveness. Take, for example, transport costs. For most industries in the United States and other developed countries, the transportation of raw materials and finished goods amounts to about 10 percent of product cost, on average. In Latin America transportation runs from 15 percent of product costs in Chile to 34 percent in Peru, mainly because of high vehicle-maintenance costs and lengthy driving times, both caused by inferior roadways. The World Bank study referred to above claims that improving the region's infrastructures, such as roadways, bridges, and tunnels, by driving down costs and hence prices of goods could result in annual gains per capita ranging from 1.4 to 1.8 percent of a country's GDP.

Safe drinking water, sanitary waste disposal, modern roadways and railways, and reliable electricity will have a marked positive impact on massive pockets of poverty throughout the region. If U.S. companies, as well as rivals from Europe and Asia, would concentrate their FDI on infrastructure projects in Bolivia, Nicaragua, Honduras, Ecuador, Guatemala, and Paraguay, enormous strides would be made over the next decade in reducing extreme poverty in these nations.

Private Participation in Infrastructure Development

Private participation in infrastructures goes by the acronym PPI. The World Bank Group's Private Participation in Infrastructure Database maintains a mountain of PPI data broken down in every conceivable way. This database measures the progress in infrastructure improvements over the fifteen-year period from 1990 through 2004 and covers projects that meet three criteria:

1. Projects that are owned or managed by private companies in low-and middle-income countries

2. Projects that directly or indirectly serve the public—captive facilities such as co-generation power plants and private telecommunications networks are excluded unless a significant share of output is sold to serve the public under a contract with a utility
3. Projects that reached financial closure (that is, completely financed or committed)

In 2004, private-sector investment financed forty-five infrastructure projects, of which sixteen were in the energy sector, two in telecom, fourteen in transport (roads, seaports, airports), and thirteen in water and sewage projects. Total PPI that year for all projects that met the three World Bank criteria was split $4.1 billion for the energy sector, $10.5 billion for telecoms, $2.8 billion for transport, and $1.4 billion for water and sewage.

Table 11-3 shows PPI in Latin America for projects meeting the World Bank criteria during the fifteen-year period from 1990 to 2004.

Table 11-3 | Private Participation in Latin American Infrastructure Improvements—1990–2004

	Number of Projects	Total Investment in Projects ($US Millions)
Brazil	280	164,919
Argentina	182	73,979
Mexico	147	65,137
Chile	100	23,006
Colombia	88	14,677
Peru	43	14,305
Venezuela	16	12,282
Bolivia	27	5,344
Panama	16	3,745
Dominican Republic	20	3,704
Guatemala	23	3,274
El Salvador	6	2,264
Jamaica	11	1,728
Uruguay	13	1,272
Honduras	10	1,037
Nicaragua	9	723
Costa Rica	22	560
Trinidad and Tobago	5	521
Paraguay	4	368
Guyana	4	238

Note: Ecuador statistics unavailable

Source: Private Participation in Infrastructure Database, World Bank Group

% Access to Electricity	% Access to Potable Water	% Access to Sanitary Sewerage
95	89	75
95	N/A	N/A
N/A	91	77
99	95	92
81	92	86
73	81	62
94	83	68
60	85	45
76	91	72
67	93	57
67	95	61
71	82	63
90	93	80
98	98	94
55	90	68
48	81	66
96	97	92
99	91	100
75	83	78
83	70	32

From 1990 to 2004, Latin America attracted infrastructure PPI of $393 billion for 1,062 projects, which accounted for 50 percent of all PPI expenditures in developing countries worldwide. Unfortunately, three-fourths of this amount was concentrated in three countries: Brazil, Argentina, and Mexico. An additional 15 percent went to Chile, Colombia, and Peru. Poorer countries lost out on much of this investment, driving their broken infrastructures even deeper in the hole. Of the $393 billion expenditures, 46 percent or $182 billion went to telecoms. Another $124 billion was spent in the energy sector, primarily electricity generation and distribution. The rest went to transport ($66 billion, mainly seaports and toll roads) and water and sewer projects ($21 billion, mostly for potable water.) Even today, the telecom industry receives the bulk of government and private investments to the detriment of electricity, water, and sanitation infrastructures.

PPI of $393 billion sounds like a lot of money to spend over fifteen years, and it is. Furthermore, Latin governments contributed another $160 billion, or about 40 percent of the private sector investment, mostly in the latter years. That amounts to more than $550 billion or half a trillion dollars. Remember that countries in Latin America were not at war with anyone during this period, so defense budgets were minuscule. Very little money was spent on education or health care. Even less went to fight crime. American donations were used in the drug wars, so that can't account for much of either public or private sector funds. Two separate authorities in official positions, one Guyanese, the other American, have argued that given the current dilapidated state of much of the region's infrastructure, a good bit of the $550 billion must have found its way into outlets other than infrastructure improvements. Perhaps. In any event, both private funds and government funding have now dropped to an alarming level just when many countries seemed to be making at least some progress. Good returns on investment notwithstanding, American companies as well as those from Europe and Asia have adopted a wait-and-see attitude until the left-leaning political air blows clear.

Even after spending $172 billion on the energy sector, public and private sectors combined, several countries still do not have satisfactory levels of electricity connections. In the top four countries, Brazil, Argentina, Mexico and Chile, nearly every household had electricity. However, the same cannot be said of countries with large indigenous populations. In Bolivia, only 60 percent of households have electricity, and in Guatemala only 67 percent of households enjoy electric light. Very poor countries fared even worse. Only 48 percent of Nicaraguan households have electricity, and 55 percent of Hondurans have it.

The region did much better in providing safe drinking water. In the two lowest-ranked countries, Peru (62 percent) and Guyana (70 percent), only the deeply rural areas are not connected to potable water. In all other countries, most of the populations do have it.

Sanitary waste disposal is a different story, with several countries well below safe standards. In Peru, only 22 percent of households are hooked up to sewer lines. In Bolivia 45 percent are connected, the Dominican Republic 57 percent, El Salvador 63 percent, Nicaragua 66 percent, and Honduras 68 percent. Moreover, being connected to sewer lines doesn't mean waste is disposed of in a sanitary fashion. In fact, throughout the region only a fraction of collected sewage is treated and disposed of properly. Instead, sub-par waste disposal plants dump untreated sewage directly into rivers, lakes, and the ocean.

Transport has also been given short shrift in the allocation of PPI funds. Many countries are so small that their roadway mileage is minuscule. Guatemala, Honduras, the Dominican Republic, Panama, El Salvador, Trinidad and Tobago, and Guyana each have less than 15,000 kilometers of roadways.

A small investment would create a huge improvement. Yet hardly anything is being done to better them.

Conversely, larger, more developed countries have substantial roadway mileage. In Brazil, nearly 2 million kilometers of roadways crisscross the nation. Mexico has more than 300,000 kilometers of roadways, and Argentina has 200,000 kilometers. Nearly 80 percent of the $66 billion of PPI allocated to transportation has already been spent in Brazil, Mexico, and Argentina, much of it on privatized toll roads, bridges, and tunnels.

The UNCTAD has come up with a matrix that groups countries according to their PPI potential and their PPI performance, as follows:

Front runners: Countries with high PPI potential and high PPI performance—Brazil, Chile, Costa Rica, the Dominican Republic, Mexico, Panama, Trinidad and Tobago

Above potential: Countries with low PPI potential but high PPI performance—Bolivia, Colombia, Ecuador, Guyana, Honduras, Jamaica, Nicaragua, Peru

Below potential: Countries with high PPI potential but low PPI performance—Argentina

Under-performing: Countries with low PPI potential and low PPI performance—El Salvador, Guatemala, Paraguay, Uruguay, Venezuela

UNCTAD defines the PPI Potential Index according to twelve variables: "GDP per capita, rate of GDP growth, percent of exports in GDP, telephone lines per 1,000 population, energy use per capita, R&D spending as percent of GDP, percent of students with tertiary education, country risk, share of world natural resources, share of world imports of parts for autos and electronics, world share of services exported, and the world share of inward investment."

PPI Performance is defined as the PPI a country receives relative to its size (for example, ratio of a country's share of global FDI inflows to its share of global GDP). A value greater than 1 indicates that a country receives more PPI than its relative economic size warrants, while a value below 1 indicates that it receives less.

These UNCTAD groupings are useful to the extent that they indicate two things: how companies regard a country as an investment location, and how successfully a country supports its PPI infrastructure projects once they are funded or committed to. These are two more pieces to the puzzle that should help you decide which country, if any, to invest in. Now let's look at FDI in Latin America from a narrower perspective: that is, from the amounts spent by U.S. companies.

Foreign Direct Investment from U.S. Companies

According to the U.S. Agency for International Development, of the $393 billion of FDI in Latin America from 1990 through 2004, U.S. companies contributed 44 percent, or $174 billion. Mexico received the lion's share of these funds, garnering 42 percent, or almost $73 billion, plus another $6.8 billion in 2005. Brazil also did fairly well, getting 25 percent or $43 billion, plus another $1.2 billion in 2005. **Table 11-4** shows the breakdown of FDI from the United States for the period 1990 to 2004.

Table 11-4 | Net U.S. Foreign Direct Investment to Latin America ($US Millions): 1990–2004

Recipient	Amount
Mexico	72,391
Brazil	42,514
Argentina	11,585
Panama	11,579
Venezuela	10,823
Chile	8,829

Jamaica	3,653
Colombia	2,965
Peru	2,261
Costa Rica	2,014
Trinidad and Tobago	1,580
Dominican Republic	1,427
El Salvador	801
Uruguay	376
Bolivia	304
Guatemala	264
Paraguay	176
Honduras	163
Guyana	72
Nicaragua	14
Ecuador	9

Source: USAID, Bureau for Latin America and the Caribbean, Selected Economic and Social Data

U.S. companies have followed the Europeans and Asians in reducing FDI to Latin America year by year. The peak for most countries was reached in 1999, when U.S. companies invested $23.3 billion. Since then steadily reduced investments resulted in a total of only $9.6 billion in 2005. Mexico hit its American FDI peak in 2001, capturing $14.2 billion or 77 percent of that year's total U.S. investment for all of Latin America.

Before deciding whether to make a direct investment in an infrastructure project, or in your own facility or business, or even if you only plan to contract with the government to work on a project, knowing which countries afford you the most freedom to run your business the way you want to run it would be very helpful. Will you have the freedom to compete in the open market? Will you have the freedom to choose how, when, and where to establish your facility and hire employees? Will your property be protected from theft and confiscation? In addition to performing a country risk assessment as described in Chapter 7, the degree of economic freedom you will have could very well be the deciding factor in choosing which country to invest in. Answering the above questions is a crucial step in making your selection and must be based on a good bit of research. Fortunately, a Canadian organization, The Fraser Institute, has done much of the job for you.

This Canadian think tank publishes an Economic Freedom in the World Annual Report, which measures the degree of economic freedom in each of 130 countries. Included in the report is an Economic Freedom of the World Index, ranking these countries in five areas:

- Size of government
- Legal structure and security of property rights
- Access to sound money
- Freedom to trade internationally
- Regulation of credit, labor, and business

Table 11-5 shows the twenty-one Latin countries ranked within Latin America and the world.

Table 11-5 | Economic Freedom of the World Index—Latin America and the World

Country	Rank—Latin America	Rank—World
Chile	1	20
Costa Rica (1)	2	30
El Salvador (1)	2	30
Jamaica (2)	3	40
Uruguay (2)	3	40
Panama (2)	3	40
Peru	4	48
Trinidad and Tobago	5	53
Guatemala (3)	6	60
Mexico (3)	6	60
Bolivia (4)	7	63
Honduras (4)	6	63
Argentina (5)	8	74
Nicaragua (5)	8	74
Paraguay (5)	8	74
Brazil	9	88
Guyana	10	90
Ecuador	11	95
Colombia	12	109
Dominican Republic	13	111
Venezuela	14	126

Note: There were five ties numbered (1), (2), (3), (4), and (5) in these rankings.

Source: The Fraser Institute, Economic Freedom of the World Index, Economic Freedom of the World 2006 Annual Report, James Gwarftney and Robert Lawson with William Easterly

Once again, Chile and Costa Rica appear in the top-five rankings. The following is for comparison purposes:

- The United States, Switzerland, and New Zealand were tied for third place.
- Hong Kong was the freest, followed by Singapore.
- The only countries less free than Venezuela were the two Congos and Myanmar (Burma), with Zimbabwe finishing dead last.

What do all these statistics tell us? Although Latin America has invoked many economic and political reforms over the past fifteen years and now enjoys a steady increase in year-to-year trade with the United States, when it comes to laying out their own money, U.S. companies have become gun shy. The leftist shift in elected Latin American administrations, anti-American rhetoric from President Chavez and others, and unfettered violence throughout the region have combined to paint a negative picture of potential returns on investment. This, combined with the further opening of China and India to FDI, puts Latin America in an unfavorable position to attract serious American investment.

In addition, very few Latin governments have stepped forward with promises of increased financial participation in infrastructure improvements. Several executives of companies that might make investments in the region if conditions were different have confided in me that their boards have no intention of pouring any major amounts of money into Latin infrastructures until public sentiment and politics shift back to reformed market economies. Despite these negative perceptions, many opportunities for investment in Latin American infrastructures beckon to American companies, provided they have the financial resources and management will to weather the risk.

Future Opportunities for U.S. Companies

Statistics are helpful for quantifying the magnitude of the region's infrastructure deficiencies. If nothing else, they indicate how badly infrastructures had deteriorated prior to the region's rebirth in 1989 and 1990. These statistics also point to where further investment is needed.

To date, two obstacles more than any others have blocked American companies from more participation in this huge market: corruption and political instability. As we've seen in previous chapters, corruption runs rampant throughout the region. Some countries aren't as bad as others, but every one of them suffers from substantial bribes and kickbacks, mostly paid to bureaucrats, but also to the military and law enforcement officials. Since all infrastructure projects are either government owned, government financed, or government approved, bureaucratic corruption must be calculated in bid prices. Just getting on the bidders' list in some countries requires surreptitious payments.

The amount of bribes and kickbacks varies, but rest assured, these are not insignificant amounts. This is where you have to be especially careful not to overstep the bounds of the Foreign Corrupt Practices Act. As discussed in previous chapters, the provisions of this act apply to large bribes or kickbacks to government officials who are high enough in the bureaucracy to make a difference as to who wins a bidding war. I suggest you get advice from counsel before venturing down this road. You can, however, control the amount of grease you're willing to pay, and this will give you at least some control over the amount of corruption you can cope with.

Political instability is another matter entirely. Obviously, you can't control the politics of a country. It's hard enough to assess the degree of political instability when doing your country risk analyses. Once you submit a bid and win, what looked like a stable environment when you started could easily turn out to be just the opposite by the time you actually begin working on the project.

Consider Bolivia. Prior to the election of President Evo Morales, the political pendulum was swinging back and forth but was at least somewhat predictable. Once Morales was elected, a vast change occurred. He immediately nationalized the natural gas industry, forcing participating private sector companies to accept operating decisions from the government, but then he reversed his position. How could you ever predict such changes in the political landscape when bids were submitted years in advance of the presidential election?

The returns on investment of Latin American infrastructure projects can be significant despite the risks of runaway corruption and political instability. If you are not willing to take these risks, you should not be in the infrastructure business. Fortunately, prime contractors on major infrastructure projects must carry the major portion of these risks. These contractors are usually very large companies, whether American, European, or Asian. While the prime contractor is directly responsible to the government and therefore is subject to the greatest risk and must pay the biggest bribes, the many subcontractors needed on a project are responsible only to their customer, the prime contractor.

With a few exceptions, U.S. companies involved in Latin infrastructure projects will not be primes. Instead, they will supply the equipment, parts, supplies, management and technical know-how, and possibly some of the labor to build the project. By working as a subcontractor, you are shielded by the prime contractor from the vagaries of corruption and political upheaval. This provides an excellent opportunity for smaller and mid-size companies to reap the benefits of infrastructure projects with very little risk.

If you do decide to enter bids for infrastructure projects or even to supply parts, labor, and know-how for such projects, you will probably have to arrange your own financing.

In that case, bear in mind that infrastructure project finance comes from an entirely different group of international organizations than export trade finance. To wrap up this discussion, let's take a brief look at some of the major players in the business of financing international projects, both infrastructure projects and non-infrastructure projects.

Financing Infrastructure Projects

Major funding for PPI projects comes from global project finance banks, development banks, the Overseas Private Investment Corporation, and United Nations agencies. Financing from these organizations runs the gamut from low risk to high risk, inexpensive to costly, and relatively simple to very complex. Several programs are only applicable to investments in specific countries. Matching available financing to a company's specific objectives tends to be the most difficult part of the entire exercise. Also, indirectly, USAID can be a big help for U.S. companies. Even though it does not actually fund private-sector projects, its recommendations carry a lot of weight with development banks, the Overseas Private Investment Corporation, and private-sector banks, which do most of the project financing.

You'll find some agencies and banks more helpful than others and offices in one city more helpful than offices of the same agency or bank in another city. Unfortunately, the size and strength of your company determines the amount of cooperation you receive; that is, the larger your company, the more assistance you'll get. Although smaller companies can also get funding, they must be more persistent.

The International Project Finance Association (IPFA), a trade association, is a good resource for keeping abreast of current events in infrastructure projects. IPFA also provides members with leads for arranging financing.

Global Project Finance Banks

Major international banks have been involved in project finance for many years. For small and mid-size companies, these international banks are much easier to contact and deal with than the United Nations or Washington. Every year, *Global Finance* magazine picks the world's best project finance banks. In 2003, the magazine chose Citigroup as the best project finance bank in Latin America. BankBoston, the Latin American division of Bank of America, is also very active throughout the region. *Global Finance* also lists the following best-bank choices:

- Royal Bank of Scotland as the best global infrastructure bank
- BNP Paribas as the best electric power bank
- West LB as the best oil and gas bank
- Citigroup as the best telecom bank

These banks were selected based on both objective and subjective material. Analyses considered a bank's quantitative performance over the past year, its market position, its innovation in doing deals, and the strength of the bank's finance teams.

I'm certain that one of the main reasons for choosing Citigroup as the best project finance bank in Latin America was that it is represented throughout the region. You'll find Citibank branches in every major and mid-sized city. As an American bank, Citibank is easy to deal with. I have personally used Citibank branches in Latin America for a variety of purposes in addition to project finance. Branch managers have been very willing to help me resolve a variety of sticky problems. They have been most helpful in providing contact information to influential bureaucrats and businesspeople. In addition to project finance, Citigroup offers a wide range of structured international products, including these:

- Global loan syndications
- Export credit agency financing for capital imports
- Cross-border leasing
- Cross-border securitization

For current listings of *Global Finance's* "The Best Banks" series, call the magazine's New York office at (212) 447-7900.

Development Banks

Development banks play a major role in financing Latin American infrastructure projects as well as FDI in agricultural, industrial, commercial, and service-oriented businesses. They remain outside the normal global banking system because their sole reason for existence is to provide medium- and long-term financing, both debt and equity, for upgrading developing nation infrastructures and business enterprises.

Development banks are not depositories. They do not engage in short-term credit or trade finance. They do not broker securities. They do not participate in the foreign exchange markets or capital markets, other than to raise capital for their loan and equity investment programs.

On the other hand, development banks are part of the Latin American financial system. Central banks exert regulatory controls over their activities. Much of their funding passes through commercial banking systems to the end user. Some development banks finance other development banks. All development banks are entwined with the World Bank and the International Monetary Fund (IMF). In fact, one of the primary activities of the IMF involves evaluating major projects and economic conditions for its stamp of approval before development banks lend funds.

Structure of Development Banking Industry

The development banking industry uses a two-pronged hierarchal structure to preserve national sovereignty, although responsibility lines do become blurred. On the one hand, bilateral development organizations operate under the jurisdiction of specific industrialized countries. Their financial support usually flows direct to the private sector though in some cases to the public sector. However, funds may flow through financial intermediaries, such as regional or country development banks or even country central banks, before reaching the end-user.

A parallel hierarchy begins with the handful of super international development banks. Each of these super banks maintains several subsidiaries and divisions within its organization to manage specific programs and types of financing. The Inter-American Development Bank (IDB), located in Washington, D.C., serves as the central bank for all in-country Latin American development banks.

In a recent change of direction, the IDB announced that it had begun a major new initiative, emphasizing entrepreneurs and private initiatives rather than bailing governments out of fiscal imprudence. The bank plans to sponsor infrastructure projects and other projects that bolster small business ". . . by offering credit, promoting financing for housing, spreading the benefits of the digital revolution, providing water and sanitation services and boosting education and productivity."

One reason for the IDB's change in direction is Washington's fear that the entire Latin American region is shifting to leftist politics. A second reason for the change is that growth in per-capita income has slowed to a trickle, a condition that bids fair warning of major social upheavals. Mark Weisbrot, co-director of the Center for Economic and Policy Research, said it all when he commented that in terms of Latin American economic expansion, "this has been the worst twenty-five years since the start of the twentieth century." He reflected on the fact that while Latin American per capita income increased 82 percent from 1960 to 1980, it grew a measly 14 percent from 1980 to 2005.

The IDB's merchant banking arm is the Inter-American Investment Corporation (IIC). The IIC's exclusive mission is to help companies in Latin America identify investment projects and potential joint venture partners and to obtain technical and financial assistance for developing those projects. The IIC also offers nonfinancial assistance in such matters as the following:

- Technical counseling for the preparation of preinvestment and feasibility studies
- Advisory services aimed at restoring the operating and financial capacity of companies requiring such assistance
- Advice on structuring privatization deals
- Identifying investment projects
- Coordinating with financial institutions for additional financing
- Assisting in the start-up of new companies

For further information about IIC programs, contact Inter-American Investment Corporation, 1350 New York Avenue NW, Washington, D.C. 20577.

Regional Development Banks

Regional development banks reside at the next level down from the super banks. The Caribbean Development Bank, serving the Caribbean Common Market, and the Central American Bank for Economic Integration, serving Central American countries, are prime examples.

A regional bank acts as a supernumerary coordinating organization that attempts to standardize, to some extent, investment evaluation criteria within its region. It oversees regional currency exchange relationships and solicits investors and investment opportunities in each of its member countries. It also provides technical assistance, when necessary, to sort out and arrange joint ventures.

Local Development Banks

At the bottom of the ladder, local development banks are responsible for the administration of loan funds. Many of these banks are privately owned by large multinational commercial banks or by a combination of local businesses and banks. Host-country governments own part or all of others. Local development banks may receive funding from a variety of sources, such as the super development banks, regional development banks, bilateral development finance organizations, private donors, United Nations organizations, local government aid programs through their central banks, foreign government aid programs, and local capital markets. Some have the authority to borrow from in-country commercial or merchant banks. Local development banks also assist in project evaluations and provide technical assistance.

Local development banks are expected not only to provide long-term financing but to play a developmental role in a national economy; that is, to act as a catalyst for promoting private-sector economic growth. According to some critics, in too many instances this has not happened. They complain that, with a few notable exceptions, managers of local development banks have acted as passive, conservative bankers, intent on supporting investments by large, well-known companies in sure-fire, well-conceived projects. They have not fulfilled their mission of acting as development bankers. Ventures have been judged on financial soundness and the ability of the investor and the project to repay the loan, rather than on how much the project will contribute to the economic development of the country.

Undoubtedly one major reason for this is that development banks are called banks, with the normal connotation of fiduciary responsibility as the primary objective. Another explanation might be that the roles of development banks in the overall economic objectives of countries are ill defined. Without a clear-cut definition of a government's social and economic objectives and the corresponding support of government bureaucrats to promote programs for achieving these ends, development banks cannot hope to fulfill a meaningful developmental role.

Each of the many local development banks has somewhat different eligibility requirements and promotes various forms of financing assistance, depending on the country and the current economic climate. Host-country attorneys, consultants, or local offices of international accounting firms are the best sources of information about possibilities for financing your project.

Overseas Private Investment Corporation

The Overseas Private Investment Corporation (OPIC) is a self-sustaining bilateral financing institution. Its primary mission is to offer U.S. businesses assistance in financing, issue insurance coverage for long-term direct investments, and provide market information through the following means:

- Direct loans or loan guarantees
- Insurance against political risk, currency inconvertibility, expropriation, war, revolution, and civil strife
- Investment missions stationed throughout the world
- Investor information service

OPIC finances up to 75 percent of three types of medium- and long-term projects:

1. Energy or energy-related projects (water systems, electric utilities, oil and gas drilling), businesses that produce products for host-country consumption, and the development of alternate energy sources
2. Projects offering significant trade benefits or infrastructure development for the host country
3. Projects sponsored by small businesses or co-ops that will have a positive impact on U.S. employment and on the economy and on the environment of the host country.

OPIC direct loans range from $200,000 to $4 million. Loan guarantees typically run from $1 million to $25 million, although they can reach $50 million or even more in some cases. OPIC also makes outright grants for feasibility studies and training programs in amounts up to $100,000. In addition, OPIC offers political risk insurance, direct loans, and loan guarantees for the financing of offshore leases; performance guarantees that contractors can use in lieu of bank guarantees; and loan guarantees for direct investments in oil and gas, oil shale, geothermal, mineral, solar, and other energy projects.

To get complete details about all OPIC programs, contact Overseas Private Investment Corporation, Information Officer, Office of External Affairs, 1100 New York Avenue, NW, Washington D.C. 20527.

U.S. Trade and Development Agency

The U.S. Department of State administers the U.S. Trade and Development Agency (USTDA). USTDA ". . . funds technical assistance and feasibility studies that support the development of modern infrastructures and fair, open trading environments. It focuses on sectors that benefit from U.S. exports."

In recent years, USTDA has funded feasibility studies that led to the development of large infrastructure projects such as airports and bridges. The agency claims that in 2005, projects emanating from its feasibility studies generated $43.10 in U.S. exports for every dollar it spent on such studies. Further information can be obtained by calling (703) 875-4357 or from the USTDA.

United Nations Programs

Two special United Nations programs should be added to the spectrum of sources for financing FDI in Latin America: the International Finance Corporation and the Multilateral Investment Guarantee Agency.

International Finance Corporation

The International Finance Corporation (IFC) is the world's largest multilateral organization, specifically structured to provide financial assistance in the form of loans and equity investments to private companies in developing countries. Its loans range from $1 million to $100 million, with the average loan being approximately $14 million. To qualify for IFC assistance, projects must benefit the economy of the host country and be profitable for both the company making the primary investment and any other investors in the project.

In addition, the IFC helps prospective foreign investors find local joint venture partners and negotiate contracts with host-country government agencies. Applications can get quite complex, so it's a good idea to get instruction directly from the IFC, at International Finance Corporation, 2121 Pennsylvania Avenue NW, Washington, D.C. 20433.

Multilateral Investment Guarantee Agency

The Multilateral Investment Guarantee Agency (MIGA), established in 1988, is an independent member of the World Bank Group. It does not fund projects, but it does provide guarantees that serve as insurance policies against the risks of currency transfer, expropriation, war and civil disturbance, and breach of contract by the host government. It also provides advisory services aimed at attracting foreign investment. MIGA offers the following types of insurance to private-sector companies:

- **Currency transfer:** Protects against losses arising from the investor's inability to convert local currency from profits, principal amounts of loans, invested capital, interest, and royalties, into foreign exchange for transfer outside the host country
- **Expropriation:** Protects against partial or total loss of investments as a result of acts by the host government

- **War and civil disobedience:** Protects against losses from damage to or the destruction or disappearance of tangible assets caused by politically motivated acts of war or civil disturbances in the host country, including revolution, insurrection, coups d'état, sabotage, and terrorism
- **Breach of contract:** Protects equity investment against losses arising from the host government's breach or repudiation of a contract with the investing company

The last item needs further clarification. Equity investments, loans, and loan guarantees made by equity holders can all be covered. Certain non-equity holdings are also eligible for inclusion, such as technical and management contracts and franchising and licensing agreements. MIGA insures up to 90 percent of the invested amount, with a $50 million limit per project. Coverages run for terms of up to fifteen years and in certain cases up to twenty years. Premium rates range from 0.3 to 1.5 percent per annum of the amount covered for each risk. Eligible projects include new investments associated with expansion, modernization, or financing restructuring. Infrastructure privatization projects are also included.

Further information can be obtained from Vice President, Guarantees, Multilateral Investment Guarantee Agency, 1818 H Street NW, Washington, D.C. 20433.

In conclusion, the more information you can gather about your particular market and its business environment before soliciting orders or committing to local facilities, the better your chances of success. And, in the end, it's far more prudent to seek assistance in matters that you may not be confident of handling than to go it alone and perhaps stumble along the way.

Despite all of Latin America's growing pains and volatility, with sufficient management motivation and resources, American businesses can and do exact significant benefits from the region. This is only the beginning. In future decades, Latin America will rise to the forefront of international trade. The globalization of financial markets and the free cross-border movement of people and materiel will make Latin America one of the premier locations for American business.

Appendix A

Export Assistance Centers

Atlanta (GA, AL, KY, TN, MS)
International Trade Programs
Sunbelt U.S. Export Assistance Center
75 Fifth Street, N.W., Ste 1055
Atlanta, GA 30308
Tel (404) 897-6089

Baltimore (MD, Northern VA, Washington, D.C.)
International Trade Programs
U.S. Export Assistance Center
300 West Pratt Street, Ste 300
Baltimore, MD 21201
Tel (410) 962-4582

Boston (ME, VT, NH, MA, CT, RI)
International Trade Programs
U.S. Export Assistance Center
World Trade Center, Ste 307
Boston, MA 02210
Tel (617) 424-5953

Charlotte (VA, NC, SC)
International Trade Programs
U.S. Export Assistance Center
521 East Morehead Street, Ste 435
Charlotte, NC 28202
Tel (704) 333-4886

Chicago (WI, IL, IN)
International Trade Programs
U.S. Export Assistance Center
200 Adams Street, Ste 2450
Chicago, IL 60606
Tel (312) 353-8065

Cleveland (OH, Western NY, Western PA, WV)
International Trade Programs
U.S. Export Assistance Center
600 Superior Avenue, Ste 700
Cleveland, OH 44114
Tel (216) 522-4731

Dallas (OK, TX, LA, AR)
International Trade Programs
North Texas U.S. Export Assistance Center
1450 Hughes Road, Ste 220
Grapevine, TX 76501
Tel (817) 310-3749

Denver (WY, UT, CO, NM)
International Trade Programs
U.S. Export Assistance Center
1625 Broadway Avenue, Ste 680
Denver, CO 80202
Tel (303) 844-6623, ext.18

Detroit (MI)

International Trade Programs

U.S. Export Assistance Center

211 West Fort Street, Ste 1104

Detroit, MI 48226

Tel (313) 226-3670

Newport Beach (Southern CA, NV, AZ, HI)

International Trade Programs

U.S. Export Assistance Center

3300 Irvine Avenue, Ste 305

Newport Beach, CA 92660

Tel (949) 660-1688, ext.115

Miami (FL)

International Trade Programs

U.S. Export Assistance Center

5835 Blue Lagoon Drive, Ste 203

Miami, FL 33132

Tel (305) 526-7425, ext. 21

Minneapolis (MN, ND)

International Trade Programs

U.S. Export Assistance Center

U.S. Small Business Administration

100 North Sixth Street, 210-C, Butler Square,

Minneapolis, MN 55403

Tel (612) 348-1642

Philadelphia (Eastern PA, DE, NJ)

International Trade Programs

U.S. Export Assistance Center

The Curtis Center

601 Walnut Street, Ste 580 West

Philadelphia, PA 19106

Tel (215) 597-6110

Portland (Southern WA, OR, Southern ID, Montana)

International Trade Programs

U.S. Export Assistance Center

One World Trade Center

121 SW Salmon Street, Ste 242

Portland, Oregon 97204

Tel (503) 326-5498

Seattle (Northern WA, AK, Northern ID)

International Trade Programs

U.S. Export Assistance Center

2601 Fourth Avenue, Ste 320

Seattle, WA 98121

Tel (206) 553-0051, ext. 228

St. Louis (SD, NE, IA, KS, Mo)

International Trade Programs

U.S. Export Assistance Center

8235 Forsyth Blvd., Ste 520

St. Louis, MO 63105

Tel (314) 425-3304

Appendix B

Small Business Administration Regional Offices

SBA Region I Office—ME, NH, VT, MA, CT, RI
10 Causeway Street, Ste 812
Boston, MA 02222-1093
Tel (617) 565-8415

SBA Region II Office—NY, NJ, VI, PR
26 Federal Plaza, Ste 3108
New York, NY 10278
Tel (212) 264-1450

SBA Region III Office—PA, MD, WV, VA
Federal Building
900 Market Street, 5th Floor
Philadelphia, PA 19107
Tel (215) 580-2807

SBA Region IV Office—TN, KY, NC, SC, MS, AL, GA, FL
233 Peachtree Street, NE, Ste 1800
Atlanta, GA 30303
Tel (404) 331-4999

SBA Region V Office—MN, WI, MI, OH, IL, IN
500 West Madison Street
Citicorp Center, Ste 1240
Chicago, IL 60661-2511
Tel (312) 353-0357

SBA Region VI Office—NM, TX, OK, AR, LA
4300 Amon Carter Blvd, Ste 108
Fort Worth, TX 76155
Tel (817) 684-5581

SBA Region VII Office—KS, NE, MO, IA
23 W. 8th Street, Ste 307
Kansas City, MO 64105-1500
Tel (816) 374-6380

SBA Region VIII Office—ND, SD, MT, WY, CO, UT
721 19th Street, Ste 400
Denver, CO 80202-2599
Tel (303) 844-0500

SBA Region IX Office—CA, NV, AZ
330 North Brand Blvd, Ste 1270
Glendale, CA 91203-2304
Tel (818) 552-3434

SBA Region X Office—WA, ID, OR, AK
2401 Fourth Ave., Ste 400
Seattle, WA 98121
Tel (206) 553-5676

Appendix C

Latin American Trade Associations in the United States

Argentina-American Chamber of Commerce
10 Rockefeller Plaza, Ste 1001
New York, NY 10020
Tel (212) 698-2238

Brazilian-American Chamber of Commerce
22 West 48th Street, Rm 404
New York, NY 10036
Tel (212) 575-9030

Brazilian-American Chamber of Commerce
80 Southwest Eighth Street, Ste 1800
Miami, FL 33130
Tel (305) 579-9030

North American Chilean Chamber of Commerce
30 Vessey Street, Ste 506
New York, NY 10007
Tel (212) 233-7776

Colombian-American Chamber of Commerce
150 Nassau Street, Ste 2015
New York, NY 10038
Tel (212) 233-7776

Colombian-American Chamber of Commerce
250 Catalonia Avenue, Ste 407
Coral Gables, FL 33134
Tel (305) 446-2542

Ecuador-American Association
150 Nassau, Ste 2015
New York, NY 10038
Tel (212) 808-0978

Guatemala-U.S. Trade Association
299 Alhambra Circle, Ste207
Coral Gables, FL 33134
Tel (305) 443-0343

Mexican Chamber of Commerce of Arizona
P.O. Box 626
Phoenix, AZ 85001
Tel (602) 252-6448

Mexican Chamber of Commerce of the County of Los Angeles
125 Paseo de La Plaza, Room 404
Los Angeles, CA 90012
Tel (310) 826-9898

U.S.-Mexico Chamber of Commerce
1211 Connecticut Avenue N.W.
Washington, D.C. 20036
Tel (202) 296-5198

Peruvian-American Association
50 West 34th Street
New York, NY 10036
Tel (212) 964-3855

Trinidad and Tobago Chamber of Commerce
c/o Trintoc Services, Ltd.
400 Madison Avenue, Room 803
New York, NY 10016
Tel (212) 759-3388

Venezuelan American Association of the United States
2332 Gallano Street
Coral Gables, FL 33134
Tel (305) 728-7042

Other U.S. Trade Associations

American Assoc. of Exporters and Importers
11 West 42nd Street
New York, NY 10036
Tel (212) 944-2230

Chamber of Commerce of the United States
International Division
1615 H Street N.W.
Washington, D.C. 20062
Tel (202) 463-5460

Council of the Americas
680 Park Avenue
New York, NY 10021
Tel (212) 628-3200

Federation of International Trade Associations
1900 Campus Commons Drive, Ste 340
Reston, VA 20191
Tel (703) 620-1588

Houston Inter-American Chamber of Commerce
510 Bering Drive, Ste 300
Houston, TX 77057
Tel (713) 975-6171

Latin American Chamber of Commerce
3512 Fullerton Avenue
Chicago, IL 60647
Tel (773) 252-5211

Latin American Manufacturers Association
419 New Jersey Avenue S.E.
Washington, D.C. 20003
Tel (202) 546-3803

National Customs Brokers & Forwarders Association of America
1200 18th Street N.W., Ste 901
Washington, D.C. 20036
Tel (202) 466-0222

National Foreign Trade Council
1625 K Street N.W.
Washington, D.C. 20006
Tel (202) 887-0278

NEXCO (formerly National Association of Export Companies)
P.O. Box 3949
Grand Central Station
New York, NY 10163
Tel (877) 291-4901

Pan American Society of the United States
680 Park Avenue
New York, NY 10021
Tel (212) 249-8950

Small Business Exporters Association

1156 15th Street N.W., Suite 1100

Washington, D.C. 20005

Tel (202) 659-9320

United States Council for International Business

1212 Avenue of the Americas

New York, NY 10036

Tel (212) 354-4480

U.S. Hispanic Chamber of Commerce

1030 15th Street N.W., Ste 206

Washington, D.C. 20005

Tel (202) 842-1212

World Trade Centers Association

60 East 42nd Street, Ste 1901

New York, NY 10165

Tel (212) 432-2626

American Chamber of Commerce Offices in Latin America

Argentina

American Chamber of Commerce in Argentina

Viamonte 1133, 8 Piso (1053)

Buenos Aires, Argentina

Tel (54-11) 4371-4500, (54-11) 4371-8400

amcham@amchamar.com.ar

U.S. Mailing Address:

Miami Commercial Center

8307 NW 68th St., Ste 1423

Miami, FL 33102-5743

Bolivia

American Chamber of Commerce of Bolivia

Avenida 6 de Agosto N° 2455

Edificio Hilda, Entre Bellisaria Salinas y Pedro Zalizar,

Piso 2, Of. 204

P.O. Box 8268, Of. 3

La Paz, Bolivia

Tel (59-12) 244-3939, (59-12) 244-3972

a.m.galindo@amchambolivia.com

Brazil (Rio de Janeiro)

American Chamber of Commerce for Brazil (Rio de Janeiro)

Praca Pio X-15, 5th Floor

Rio de Janeiro—RJ, Brazil 20040-020

Tel (55-21) 3213-9200, (55-21) 3213-9201

foxtrail@amchamrio.com.br

Brazil (São Paulo)

American Chamber of Commerce for Brazil (São Paulo)

Rua da Paz, no 1431, 04713-001 —Chácara Santo Antonio

São Paulo—SP, Brazil

Tel (55-11) 3011-6000 (55-11) 5180-3777

vasco@amcham.com.br

Chile

Chilean-American Chamber of Commerce

Av. Pdte. Kennedy 5735, Of. 201,

Torre Poniente, Las Condes

P.O. Box Casilla 82, Santiago 34

Santiago, Chile

Tel (562) 290-9700, (562) 212-0515

amcham@amchamchile.cl

Colombia

Colombian-American Chamber of Commerce

Calle 98, #22-64, Oficina 1209

Apartado Aereo 8008

Bogotá, Colombia

Tel (571) 621-5042 /7925, (571) 621-6838

direct@amchamcolombia.com.co

Costa Rica

Costa Rican-American Chamber of Commerce

P.O. Box 4946, 1000

San Jose, Costa Rica

Tel (506) 220-2200, (506) 220-2300

chamber@amcham.co.cr

U.S. Mailing Address:

Costa Rican-American Chamber of Commerce

SJ01576

P.O. Box 02516

Miami, Fl 33102-5216

Dominican Republic

American Chamber of Commerce of the Dominican
Republic

Av. Sarasota No. 25

Torre Empresarial 6to. Piso

Santo Domingo, Dominican Republic

Tel (809) 381-0777, (809) 381-0303

amcham@verizon.net.do

U.S. Mailing Address:

AMCHAM

EPS A-528

P.O. Box 02-5256

Miami, FL 33102

Ecuador (Guayaquil)

Ecuadorian-American Chamber of Commerce
(Guayaquil)

Ave. Francisco de Orellana y Alberto Borges, Edificio
Centrum, Piso 6, Of. 5

Guayaquil, Ecuador

Tel (59-34) 269-3470/71/72/73/74 or (59-34)
269-3465

director@amchamecuador.org

Ecuador (Quito)

Ecuadorian-American Chamber of Commerce (Quito)

Edificio Multicentro, Piso 4

La Niña y Avda. 6 de Diciembre

Quito, Ecuador

Tel (59-32) 250-7450, (59-32) 250-4571

vdelapaz@ecamcham.com

El Salvador

American Chamber of Commerce of El Salvador

Edificio World Trade Center Torre II

Local 308, 89 Avenida Norte, Col. Escalón

San Salvador, El Salvador

Tel (503) 263-9494, (503) 263-9393

ebettaglio@amchamsal.com

Guatemala

American Chamber of Commerce in Guatemala

5 Avenida 5-55, Zona 14

Torre I, Nivel 5, Europlaza

Guatemala City 01014, Guatemala

Tel (502) 2333-3899, (502) 2368-3536

director@amchamguate.com

U.S. Mailing Address:

AmCham Guatemala

ID07-0120

P.O. Box 440999

Miami, FL 33126-1009

Honduras

Honduran-American Chamber of Commerce

Hotel Honduras Maya

Apartado Postal 1838

Tegucigalpa, Honduras

Tel (504) 232-6035, (504) 232-2031

amcham1@honduras.quik.com

Jamaica

American Chamber of Commerce of Jamaica

Jamaica Pegasus Hotel, Rm. #127

81 Knutsford Blvd.

Kingston 5, Jamaica

Tel (876) 929-7866/7867 or (876) 929-8597

amcham@cwjamaica.com

Mexico

American Chamber of Commerce of Mexico

A.C., Lucerna 78-4

06600 Mexico, D.F., Mexico

Tel (52-55) 5141-3800, (52-55) 5703-3908/
5566-6274

amchammx@amcham.com.mx

U.S. Mailing Address:

P.O. Box 60326

Houston, TX 77205-0326

Nicaragua

American Chamber of Commerce of Nicaragua

Apartado Postal 2720

Managua, Nicaragua

Tel (505) 267-3099, (505) 267-3098

amcham@amchamnic.org.ni

Panama

American Chamber of Commerce and Industry of
Panama

Apartado Postal 0843-00152

Panama, Rep. de Panama

Tel (507) 301-3881, (507) 301-3882

amcham@panamcham.com

Paraguay

Paraguayan-American Chamber of Commerce

25 de mayo 2090

Edif. Mayor Bullo

Asunción, Paraguay

Tel (595) (21) 22 19 26 or (595) (21) 22 15 25 or (595)
(21) (595) (21) 22 19 26 or (595) (21) 22 21 60

pamcham@pamcham.com.py

Peru

American Chamber of Commerce of Peru

Av. Ricardo Palma 836

Miraflores

Lima 18, Peru

Tel (511) 241-0708, (511) 241-0709

adefilippi@amcham.org.pe

Trinidad And Tobago

American Chamber of Commerce of Trinidad & Tobago

P.O. Bag 150

Newtown, Port of Spain, Trinidad & Tobago, W.I.

Tel (868) 622-4466/0340, (868) 628-9428

Uruguay

Chamber of Commerce Uruguay-USA

Plaza Independencia 831

Oficina 209, Edificio Plaza Mayor

11100 Montevideo, Uruguay

Tel (59-82) 908-9186, (59-82) 908-9187

maonzo@ccuruguayusa.com

Venezuela

American Chamber of Commerce & Industry

Torre Credival, Piso 10

2da. Avenida de Campo Alegre

Campo Alegre Apartado 5181

Caracas 1010-A, Venezuela

Tel (58-221) 263-0833, (58-212)
263-1829/0586/2060

U.S. Mailing Address:

VenAmCham

S-522, Jet Internacional C.A.

P.O. Box 020010

Miami, FL 33102-0010

Appendix E

Bi-National Chambers of Commerce in Florida

Association of Bi-National Chambers of Commerce in Florida
260 Crandon Blvd, Ste 32 PMB 136
Key Biscayne, FL 33149
Tel (305) 365-7247

Argentine-Florida Chamber of Commerce
1901 Brickell Avenue, Ste B-201
Miami, FL 33129
Tel (305) 858-1516

Costa Rica U.S. Chamber of Commerce
7930 S.W. 20 Street
Miami, FL 33155
Tel (305) 266-4849

Colombian-American Chamber of Commerce
250 Catalonia Avenue Office, Ste 407
Coral Gables, FL 33134
Tel (305) 446-2542

Dominican-American Chamber of Commerce
2828 N.W. 17th Avenue
Miami, FL 33142
Tel (305) 635-4511

Dominican International Chamber of Commerce, Inc.
104 SW 9th Street, Ground Floor
Miami, FL 331030
Tel (305) 643-5535

The Ecuadorian American Business Association
555 N.E. 15th Street, Ste 12 B
Miami, FL 33132
Tel (305) 562-7438

Jamaica USA Chamber of Commerce, Inc.
4770 Biscayne Boulevard, Ste 1050
Miami, FL 33137
Tel (305) 576-7888

Nicaraguan American Chamber of Commerce
175 Fontainebleau Blvd., Ste 1R-10
Miami, FL 33172
Tel (305) 599-2737

Peruvian American Trade Center
1940 N.W. 82nd Avenue
Miami, FL 33126
Tel (305) 728-6272

Uruguayan-American Chamber of Commerce
1077 Ponce de Leon Blvd., Ste B
Coral Gables, FL 33134
Tel (305) 476-8169

Venezuelan American Chamber of Commerce
2332 Galiano Street, 2nd floor
Coral Gables, FL 33134
Tel (305) 728-7042

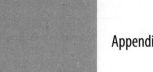

Appendix F

Internet Addresses

Federal Government

Agent/Distributor Service
www.unzco.com

Bureau of the Census
www.census.gov

Bureau of Economic Analysis
www.bea.gov

Bureau of Industry and Security
www.bis.doc.gov

Bureau of Public Affairs, Department of State
www.state.gov/r/pa/

Department of Commerce
www.commerce.gov

Economic Development Administration
www.eda.gov

Economics and Statistics Administration
www.esa.doc.gov and www.home.stat-usa.gov

Export.gov
www.export.gov

Export-Import Bank of the United States (Eximbank)
www.exim.gov

Export Trading Company Affairs
www.trade.gov/td/oetca/index.html

Foreign Agriculture Service (Department of Agriculture)
www.fas.usda.gov

Globus & USCS
www.stat-usa.gov/tradtest.nsf

International Catalog Exhibition Program
www.export.gov/comm_svc/cata log_program.html

International Company Profile
www.export.gov/comm_svc/intl_co_ profile.html

International Trade Administration
www.trade.gov

Latin American Trade Associations in the United States
www.sba.gov/oit/txt/info/Guide-To-Exporting/trad21.html

Market Access and Compliance Office
www.trade.gov/mac

Minority Business Development Agency
www.mbda.gov

National Institute of Standards and Technology
www.nist.gov

National Technical Information Service
www.ntis.gov

Office of Technology Policy
www.technology.gov/otpolicy

National Oceanic & Atmospheric Administration
www.noaa.gov

National Telecommunications and Information Administration
www.ntia.gov

National Trade Data Bank
www.stat-usa.gov/tradtest.nsf
www.ita.doc.gov/td/sif/how_do_i_ go_global.htm

Office of Small and Disadvantaged Business Utilization/Minority Resource Center
www.usaid.gov/business/ small_business

Office of Trade and Industry, Manufacturing Services, International Trade Administration
www.ita.doc.gov/td/industry/otea/

Overseas Private Investment Corporation
www.opic.gov

Patent and Trademark Office
www.uspto.gov

Small Business Administration
www.sba.gov

SBA Export Assistance Centers
www.sba.gov/oit/export/useac.html

SBA Office of International Trade
www.sba.gov/oit/finance/index.html

SBA Regional Offices
www.sba.gov

Service Corps of Retired Executives
www.score.org

Technology Administration
www.technology.gov

Trade Compliance Center
www.tcc.export.gov

United States Agency for International Development
www.usaid.gov

USAID, Bureau for Latin America and the Caribbean, Selected Economic and Social Data
www.usaid.gov/locations/latin_america_caribbean/

USAID, Office of Small and Disadvantaged Business, Utilization/Minority Resource Center
www.usaid.gov/business/small_business/

United States Commercial Service
www.buyusa.gov

United States Trade and Development Agency
www.tda.gov/ustda

United Nations And Other International Public-Sector Agencies

Inter-American Development Bank
www.iadb.org

Inter-American Investment Corp.
www.iic.int

International Finance Corporation
www.ifc.org

International Monetary Fund
www.imf.org

Multilateral Investment Guarantee Agency
www.miga.org

Organization for Economic Cooperation and Development
www.oecd.org

UN Conference on Trade and Development
www.unctad.org

UN Economic Commission for Latin America and the Caribbean
www.eclac.cl

World Bank
www.worldbank.org

World Trade Organization
www.wto.org

Trade Pacts And Legislation Addresses

Bolivarian Alternative for Latin America and the Caribbean
www.alternativebolivariana.org

Caribbean Community
www.caricom.org

Dominican Republic-Central American Free Trade Agreement
www.fas.usda.gov/itp/CAFTA/cafta.html

Foreign Corrupt Practices Act
www.usdoj.gov/criminal/fraud/fcpa/dojdocb.htm

Free Trade Area of the Americas
www.ftaa-alca.org/alca_e.asp

North American Free Trade Agreement
www.ustr.gov/trade_agreements/regional/NAFTA/section_index.html

Sarbanes-Oxley Act of 2002
www.sarbanes-oxley.com

Summit of the Americas
www.summit-americas.org

Publications

Advertising Age
www.adage.com

The Basic Guide to Exporting
www.unzco.com/basicguide

The CIA World Fact Book
www.cia.gov/cia/publications/factbook

Commercial News USA
www.thinkglobal.us

Current History
www.currenthistory.com

Doing Business in 2006: Creating Jobs (report from the International Finance Corporation)
www.doingbusiness.org

The Economist
www.economist.com

Foreign Affairs
www.foreignaffairs.org

Global Entertainment and Media Outlook: 2005-2009, (report from PriceWaterhouseCoopers)
www.pwc.com

Global Finance
www.gfmag.com

The Industrial Outlook (a report from the Department of Commerce)
www.ita.doc.gov/td/industry/otea/outlook

Journal of Commerce
www.joc.com

Latin Business Chronicle
www.latinbusinesschronicle.com

LatinFinance
www.latinfinance.com

Latin Trade
www.latintrade.com

Market Research Reports (from the Department of Commerce)
www.export.gov/marketresearch.html

Trafficking in Persons Report 2006 (from the Department of State)
www.state.gov/g/tip/rls/tiprpt/2006/

World Trade
www.worldtrademag.com

Private-Sector Organizations

ATA Carnet Department, U.S. Council for International Business
www.uscib.org

Association of American Chambers of Commerce in Latin America
www.aaccla.org

Argentina, www.amachamar.co.ar

Bolivia, www.amchambolivia.com

Brazil (Rio de Janeiro),
www.amchamrio.com.br

Brazil (São Paulo),
www.amcham.com.br

Chile, www.amchamchile.cl

Colombia,
www.amachamcolombia.com.co

Costa Rica, www.amcham.co.cr

Dominican Republic, www.amacham.org.do/english.htm

Ecuador (Guayaquil),
www.amchamecuador.org

Ecuador (Quito), www.ecamcham.com

El Salvador, www.amchamsal.com

Guatemala, www.amchamguate.com

Honduras,
www.amchamhonduras.org

Jamaica, www.amchamjamaica.org

Mexico, www.amcham.com.mx

Nicaragua, www.amchamnic.org.ni

Panama, www.panamcham.com

Paraguay, www.pamcham.com.py

Peru, www.amcham.org.pe

Trinidad and Tobago,
www.amchamtt.com

Uruguay, www.ccuruguayusa.com

Venezuela, www.venamcham.org

American Association of Exporters and Importers
www.aaei.org

Argentine-Florida Chamber of Commerce
www.argentinaflorida.com

Association of Bi-National Chambers of Commerce in Florida
www.abicc.org

Brazilian-American Chamber of Commerce
www.brazilcham.com

Center for Economic and Policy Research
www.cepr.net

Chamber of Commerce of the United States
www.uschamber.org

Colombian-American Chamber of Commerce
www.colombiachamber.com

Council of the Americas
www.counciloftheamericas.org

Dominican International Chamber of Commerce
www.dicchamberusa.org

Ecuadorian American Business Association
www.yeap.us

Federation of International Trade Associations
www.fita.org

Fraser Institute
www.freetheworld.com

Global Offset and Countertrade Association
www.globaloffset.org

International Chamber of Commerce
www.iccwbo.org

International Forfaiting Association
www.forfaiters.org

International Project Finance Association
www.ipfa.org

Jamaican USA Chamber of Commerce, Inc.
www.jamaicausachamber.org

Latin American Chamber of Commerce
www.latinamericanchamberofcom
merce.com

Latin American Trade Council of
Oregon (LATCO)
www.latco.org

National Customs Brokers & Forwarders Association of America, Inc.
www.ncbfaa.org

National Foreign Trade Council
www.nftc.org

NEXCO (formerly National Association
of Export Companies)
www.nexco.org

Nicaraguan American Chamber of
Commerce
www.nacc-miami.com

Peruvian-American Association
www.peruvianamericanchamber.org

Peruvian American Trade Center
www.peruviantradecenter.org

Small Business Exporters Association
(not part of the SBA)
www.sbea.org

Transparency International
www.transparency.org

United States Council for International
Business
www.uscib.org

U.S. Hispanic Chamber of Commerce
www.ushcc.com

U.S.–Mexico Chamber of Commerce
www.usmcoc.org

Venezuelan American Chamber of
Commerce
www.venezuelanchamber.org

World Economic Forum (Geneva,
Switzerland)
www.weforum.org

World Trade Centers Association
www.world.wtca.org

World Vision International
www.wvi.org

Private-Sector Companies

American International Group, Inc.
www.aig.com

Baker & McKenzie
www.bakernet.com

British American Forfaiting Company
of St. Louis
www.british-americanforfaiting.com

Creative Capital Associates
www.ccassociates.com

Corporation for International Business
www.atacarnet.com

Economist Intelligence Unit
www.eiu.com

eLease International, Inc.
www.eleaseinternational.com

Factors Chain International
www.factors-chain.com

FCIA Management Company (formerly
Foreign Credit Insurance Association)
www.fcia.com

First Commercial Credit
www.1stcommrcialcredit.com

First International Merchant Bank of
Malta (formerly London Forfaiting Co.
New York)
www.fimbank.com

International Company Profiles
www.icpcredit.com

International Factors
www.ifgroup.com

International SOS Assistance
www.internationalsos.com

InternetLC.com
www.Internetlc.com

Internet World Stats
www.Internetworldstats.com

Kroll Latin American & Caribbean
Headquarters
www.krollworldwide.com

LeaseForce International
www.leaseforce.com

mosaic International
www.mosaicinternational.com

Private Export Funding Corporation
www.pefco.com

Standard Bank of South Africa
www.standardbank.co.za

Trade and Export Finance Online
www.tefo.com

Travel Assistance International
www.travelassistance.com

ZenithOptimedia
www.zenithoptimedia.com

North Atlantic Ocean

Washington

Mexico

Gulf of Mexico

Havana

Bahamas

Cuba

Mexico City

Belize

Jamaica

Puerto Rico

Haiti

Dom. Rep.

St. Kitts & Nevis

Antigua & Barbuda

Dominica

Guatemala

Honduras

Nicaragua

Caribbean Sea

St Lucia

El Salvador

Panama

Costa Rica

St Vincent & the Grenadines

Grenada

Barbados

Caracas

Trinidad & Tobago

Venezuela

Paramaribo

Georgetown

French Guiana

Bogota

Suriname

Quito

Colombia

Guyana

Ecuador

Peru

Brazil

Lima

La Paz

Bolivia

Brasilia

Sucre

Paraguay

Chile

Asuncion

Uruguay

Santiago

Buenos Aires

Montevideo

Argentina

South Atlantic Ocean

Falkland Islands

South Georgia

Index